JB-R
Hiebert
   Franklin Delano Roosevelt

c.3

FRANKLIN DELANO ROOSEVELT

PRESIDENT FOR THE PEOPLE

Immortals of History

JB-R

FRANKLIN DELANO ROOSEVELT

PRESIDENT FOR THE PEOPLE

by

Roselyn and Ray Eldon Hiebert

FRANKLIN WATTS, INC.
575 Lexington Avenue
New York, N.Y. 10022

First Printing
Library of Congress Catalog Card Number: 68-15570
Copyright © 1968 by Franklin Watts, Inc.
Printed in the United States of America

For

David and Steven

CONTENTS

FRANKLIN
DELANO ROOSEVELT

PRESIDENT FOR THE PEOPLE

PROLOGUE

Franklin Delano Roosevelt (1882–1945) was the thirty-second President of the United States of America. For an unprecedented four terms he held the Presidency, serving from 1933 to 1945, longer than any other man before him. Probably no other man will ever serve as long again. For after Roosevelt's death a constitutional amendment was passed that limited the Presidency to two elected terms.

Certainly, he was among the most powerful Presidents America has had. He was swept into office by an overwhelming majority, and through the Depression and war, maintained his popular support in four Presidential campaigns, despite increasing undercurrents of opposition and criticism.

He chose to be a man of the people. The little man, the man on the street, factory workers, farmers, members of minority groups—these people gave him their support, and it was this popularity that provided the base for his strength and power.

He led the nation through two of the greatest

3

crises in its history. He came to the White House at the peak of the world's worst depression and sponsored new programs to bring the country back to economic health. He served in an era when world forces were in upheaval, leading ultimately to the largest war man has known. As Commander in Chief of the American forces during World War II, he joined with the Allies and helped lead democracy to victory.

Most important, he pushed America into the twentieth century. He understood the urgent need for new economic ideas and social programs. He realized the new force of mass communication and the power of public opinion. He saw the need for strong federal government planning for the good of the common man. He pulled America into a new era of internationalism, global commitments, world government, and the United Nations.

Although he was a President for the people, he himself was an uncommon man. He was, above all else, an aristocrat, a gentleman from the estates of the Hudson, his ancestors dating to the earliest European settlements of the New World. He was Groton prepared, Harvard educated, and broadly traveled.

His aristocracy was peculiarly American. His wealth and position were a stewardship, requiring duties and responsibilities that meant hard work, faithfulness, and care. He was taught that mankind was basically good, that the world was making progress, and that those who were fortunate had an obligation to preserve goodness and move the world forward.

As a Roosevelt, he was reared with a sense of his own importance. Some mistook his determination to fulfill his role as arrogance and hunger for power. From an early age his ambition was to be President of the United States, like his cousin Theodore. He strove to keep this rendezvous with his destiny.

He was, finally, a man of courage, for he overcame the greatest physical odds through will and determination to rise to prominence and power. At the peak of his manhood, he was stricken with polio, paralyzed from the waist down, his legs withered and useless, his career shattered. Many people felt he should retire to Hyde Park as an invalid and a gentleman. But he forced himself to resume a normal life, and, in spite of his crippling disease, became a leader of the nation and the world.

CHAPTER ONE
★★★★★★

AN ARISTOCRATIC BEGINNING

One day in the mid-1640's a young Dutchman rowed to the shore of an uncivilized island called New Amsterdam, then inhabited mostly by Indians, wild animals, and a few Dutch settlers. Little did he realize that someday New Amsterdam would be New York, the largest city of the most powerful nation on earth. And little did he dream that he would be the founding father of one of his new country's most important families and the ancestor of two American Presidents, Theodore and Franklin Delano Roosevelt.

The young Dutchman was Claes Martenszen van Rosenvelt, whose name meant Nicholas, son of Martin of the Rose Field. He had sailed for fifty days to cross the Atlantic to the New World. The family he had left behind were people of substance of Oud-Vossemer on Tholen, Holland. In that village today the crest of the Roosevelts still hangs. It is a knight's silver shield with a trio of red roses growing from a

7

spot of greensward and bears the words *Qui Plan-tavit Curabit*, "He who sows shall reap."

Like many immigrants to the New World, Claes found that his name was long and cumbersome, so he simplified it to Claes van Rosenvelt. He married a Dutch settler's daughter and cleared a forty-eight-acre farm on the island of New Amsterdam, where he raised five children and prospered. His oldest son further changed the family name, perhaps because of bad handwriting. He became known as Nicholas Roosevelt, and that was the spelling used by the family thereafter.

Nicholas set up a small wheat-grinding mill on the waterfront and became a merchant, the first of a long line of Roosevelt businessmen. His sons followed him in business, and it was their successful real estate dealings that formed the basis of the Roosevelt wealth. One of his sons sired the Theodore Roosevelt branch of the family, and another founded the Franklin side.

In the fourth generation, Isaac Roosevelt, great-grandson of Claes and great-great-grandfather of Franklin, was known as the first American Roosevelt because of his active role in colonial and revolutionary politics. A successful merchant, he joined the side of the colonists in the Revolutionary War and served as a state senator. He established the first large sugar refinery on Manhattan Island and be-

came president of the second bank to be organized in the new country.

In the late 1700's and early 1800's the fifth, sixth, and seventh generations of Franklin Roosevelt's branch of the family lived genteel lives as merchants and farmers on pastoral estates along the banks of the Hudson River. Investments in real estate and business enterprises provided enough substance for college educations, foreign travel, and the lives of country squires.

Franklin Roosevelt's father, James, was born in 1828. He was graduated from Union College in 1847 and took a degree in law from Harvard in 1851. He married Rebecca Howland in 1853, and they had one son, James Roosevelt Roosevelt, called Rosy, who was Franklin's half-brother and older than the future President by twenty-eight years.

Instead of law, Franklin's father followed the family pattern and chose a career in business. He inherited an interest in coal and transportation, eventually becoming vice-president of the Delaware and Hudson Canal Company and president of some smaller business ventures. With an uncle, William Henry Aspinwall, he helped build the Consolidated Coal Company into one of the largest coal combinations in the country. But his enterprises were frequently unsuccessful, especially during the years of inflation and depression after the Civil War. He was voted out

of control of the coal business, lost much of his investment in a southern railroad company, and failed in a venture to build a canal in Nicaragua.

In the mid-1870's James Roosevelt's first wife, Rebecca, died, leaving him alone at his Hyde Park estate. Four years later he met a young girl who was the same age as his son Rosy. She was Sara Delano, daughter of an old family that lived at Algonac, the Delano estate just twenty miles from Hyde Park. Sara was well educated and broadly traveled. Her ancestors were sea merchants and naval captains, and the family now lived along the Hudson as the Roosevelts did.

Sara Delano was slim, tall, and charming. She had grown up in a pleasant family of eleven children where reading aloud, sewing, flower arranging, sports, social calls, and strict church attendance were the usual routine. She was twenty-six years old and James Roosevelt was fifty-two when they first met. She was attracted by the widower's courtly manner, worldly understanding, and tender humor. Her father, Warren Delano, objected strenuously to their friendship because of the difference in age, but they fell in love and their courtship led to marriage in 1880.

Monday, January 30, 1882, dawned cold and windy. Along the rolling Palisades of the Hudson River the look of snow hung in the air. At Springwood, the Roosevelt home at Hyde Park, the birth of

the firstborn was near. All through the day anxious servants hurried about their tasks in expectation, and James Roosevelt waited with concern while his young wife began labor pains. At last, at about nine in the evening, everyone gave a sigh of relief when the first thin cries of the new baby were heard. With the dignity typical of the Roosevelts, the proud father sat down before his wife's diary and wrote, "A quarter to nine my Sallie had a splendid large baby boy. He weighs 10 lbs., without clothes."

They called the new infant "Baby" for several months until they could decide which family tradition to follow, Roosevelt or Delano. The Delanos won, finally, when the baby was christened Franklin Delano Roosevelt on March 29, 1882, at the St. James Episcopal Church in Hyde Park. Sara had wanted to name her son after her father, Warren Delano, who had died recently, but her brother's son had already been given that name so she chose the name of an uncle, Franklin Delano. She thus broke a Roosevelt tradition of naming Roosevelt sons for Roosevelts. She often said later that Franklin was more a Delano than a Roosevelt.

Life at Hyde Park was calm and efficient. Springwood was a lovely home for a new family and a splendid place for a son to be born. Everything seemed to revolve around young Franklin. He was robust and easy to care for, and the servants adored him. His mother focused her entire energies on him; there were no siblings to compete for her affections, and no other pressing duties to be done.

Sara hovered protectively over her son. She breast-fed him for almost a year and bathed him herself. Until he was five, she dressed him in girls' clothes and let his hair grow in long, shoulder-length curls. After dresses, he graduated to kilts of Murray plaid and Little Lord Fauntleroy suits. He grew to dislike his "sissy" clothes, and when he was eight, finally persuaded his mother to give him his first sailor suit. But he was so protected that, when he was eight and a half, taking his first bath alone was such an event that he had to write to his father about it.

His father, on the other hand, wanted Franklin to be a sportsman, to love nature and outdoor activity. While Franklin was still very young, his father would take him for rides around the estate. James Roosevelt was a true Hudson Valley patroon. With his sideburns neatly brushed, riding boots polished and spurred, bowler hat squarely in place, and riding crop in hand, he would call for Franklin and they would set out on a daily inspection tour of the fields and forests, formal gardens, greenhouse, grapery, ice houses, barns, and stables.

From his father, Franklin acquired a lifelong interest in sports, nature, horses, sailing, and an active life. From his mother he acquired a self-confidence at times almost bordering on egotism, but also a sense of his own destiny, a feeling that he was important and had a special mission, giving him a drive to accomplish what others could not. He was close to his mother as long as she lived, and he corresponded with her frequently wherever he was.

As though aware of her son's destiny, Sara carefully treasured Franklin's every letter, from his first note painfully penned in ink with illustrations of sailboats, written when he was five. She preserved each document. She kept an elaborate diary in which she recorded his many activities. She even saved his clothes, wrapping his socks, shoes, shirts, and dresses in carefully labeled packages.

One of Franklin's first letters to his mother was about sledding with his father. They often tobogganed together on the snowy slope toward the river behind the South Porch, or they would iceboat on the frozen Hudson. After one such outing, when he was five, he wrote:

My dear mama
We coasted! yesterday nothing dangerous yet, look for tomorrow!

your boy

Another of his first letters thanked her for a set of soldiers. "We have battles with the soldiers every day, and they are so nice," he wrote. Shortly after, in 1888, he showed an early interest in birds.

My dear mama,

    *I am in a great hurry. I found two birds nests.
I took one egg   we are all well. I am going to the
Millie Rogers Party. and to meet Papa. Good bye
your loving*

Franklin

P S   love to all

In another letter he told of his summer activities.

My dear mamma

    *I went fishing yesterday after noon with papa
we caught a dozen of minnows   we left them on
the bank   papa told me it would frighten the fish to
put them in the pond   how is dear grandpapa   I
hope he is better   dear mama I send you a kiss   your
loving son*

Franklin

    Perhaps one reason he wrote to his mother more
often than other children was that Sara and James
were often away on trips. Though Sara adored her
only child, she was also a devoted wife. She left
Franklin in the secure hands of his nurse and the
Scottish maid while she joined her husband in New
York to attend the opera or a party or a ball. Since
James had railroad interests, she also accompanied
him on lengthy railroad inspection trips. When
Franklin was four, she left for three months to tour
Mexico and California. She returned with the gift of
a hobbyhorse, which Franklin promptly named Mex-
ico.

Sometimes Franklin went along with his parents. When he was one, he joined the family for the summer at Campobello Island where James had built a summer home. When he was only three he traveled to Europe, the first of many trips since it was the Roosevelt custom to live abroad for a few months of every year. He traveled to Europe eight times during his first fourteen years.

On his first trip across the Atlantic, the Roosevelt family traveled on the *Germanic*. The ship ran into heavy seas on Easter morning. Waves pounded at the ship, causing damage, knocking the captain unconscious, and smashing the bulkhead over the Roosevelt cabin. Water poured in and rose higher and higher. Sara was sure it was the end. She wrapped her fur coat around little Franklin and said to her husband, "Poor little boy. If he must go down he is going down warm." But Franklin was more concerned with his toys. He cried out, "Mama, Mama, save my jumping jack." Avoiding disaster, the vessel returned safely to England for repairs.

Life at Hyde Park was more serene and sheltered, but Franklin was given responsibilities early in life. At five his parents gave him an Irish Setter puppy. He had to take care of the puppy—feed, housebreak, train, and groom him. His father said, "I want him to have pets, but he must learn that a dog or a pony is not just another plaything, to be cast aside and forgotten when his attention is attracted to something else. The way to teach him is to make him take care of them himself."

On his seventh birthday, Franklin was given Debby, his prized pony. He fed and watered her, exercised and groomed the pony and cleaned her stall under the careful supervision of the family coachman. He often rode Debby across the meadows and fields and followed the adults when they rode to hounds. By the summer he was eight, Franklin rode from Hyde Park to Algonac, twenty miles away.

Franklin had an early introduction to all kinds of important people. His parents entertained and visited many notables. When Franklin was five and his family was in Washington, he paid his first visit to the White House. When he stepped up to be introduced to President Cleveland, the President said, "My boy, I am making a strange wish for you. I hope you will never be President of the United States."

Though Franklin spent a good deal of his time with adults and was rather shy and self-conscious with strangers, he did have the companionship of some children. A mile away was the Archibald Rogers estate, and Colonel Rogers' sons, Archie and Edmund, were his close playmates. When quite small the boys rigged up a platform with an old piece of canvas and a toy cannon in a tall tree near Franklin's house. They pretended they were sailing an American man-of-war over the seven seas.

During the summertime they built rafts and swam in the old swimming hole at the Rogers estate. With Edmund, or more often alone, Franklin climbed the old apple tree, dug into woodchuck holes, or sprawled flat in the strawberry patch and stuffed himself with berries. In winter Edmund sometimes joined him to sail toy boats in the melting snow puddles, or they would dash to the river to ice-skate, iceboat, play hockey at the Rogers' pond, or build elaborate tunnels in the snow.

Sometimes Franklin entertained children at home. Once his godfather's daughter, Eleanor, spent the afternoon riding around the floor on Franklin's back. Little did he realize that someday he would marry her. Since Franklin did not have the competition of brothers and sisters and most often spent his time with adults, he sometimes had trouble getting along with other children. He tended to be a leader and ordered his playmates around. Once when his mother scolded him for this, Franklin replied, "Mummie, if I didn't give the orders, nothing would happen."

Discipline was no problem in raising Franklin. His parents had a firm belief that they should reason with their son and make logical rules, which they explained carefully and expected him to obey. Franklin flourished under this treatment. He was treated as an adult and was never subjected to rules solely for their own sake. He had a desire to please. His parents always took secret pride in the easy management of their son.

Once, however, he was disciplined for an infraction, and it almost broke his heart. When he was eleven, he received his first shotgun. He valued it highly as he had already begun collecting birds. Out on an expedition one spring day, he and his mother were tramping through the woods when the shotgun accidentally discharged. Franklin had been carefully instructed by his father on using the safety catch. Luckily the shot hit the ground and no one was injured, but the gun was taken away from the heartsick boy for an entire year.

He seldom rebelled against this type of discipline, but once in a while his stubborn Dutch streak would appear. At Campobello, the summer he was nine, he decided he wanted more freedom to make his own decisions. He informed his parents he was going to eat, sleep, and play when he wanted to. His parents were startled but agreed and set him free from his strict routine. They did not ask him what he had done at the end of his day of freedom and made no comment when the next day Franklin returned without argument to his rigorous schedule.

His way of manipulating his parents was usually more subtle than outright disobedience. To avoid attending Sunday school he would frequently come down with what his father called a Sunday headache. And when his mother insisted on piano and drawing lessons for him, he often made complaints that his hand hurt a little or that he had a slight cut.

As a lad, Franklin was a high-spirited boy of abounding vitality. He appeared to be healthy but he did have the childhood disease of chickenpox and a serious case of typhoid fever when he was seven. He was also a frequent victim of severe colds and fever.

He was most interested in outdoor pursuits, especially bird watching. His lifelong interest in birds began when he was ten years old. Soon he knew the name of almost every bird in the neighborhood and could recognize their calls. He carried a notebook on his walks through the woods and made careful observations of the birds he saw. He decided to make a collection of birds of Dutchess County, something no one had ever done before. Franklin promised his parents he would never kill more than one bird of each species and would never kill one in nesting season. He soon shot his first crow with his rifle and decided to skin and stuff his own specimens. The nasty chore made him ill, but he stubbornly refused to give up until he could perform the job well. Only then did he consent to send his catches to a taxidermist for stuffing.

Within a short time birds were everywhere in the house. Before Franklin's fourteenth birthday he had preserved more than three hundred species, the most complete collection made up to that time in Dutchess County. The birds were put on display in cabinets in the entrance hall of the house.

Franklin was a born collector. In addition to birds, he avidly collected stamps. His mother had given him a rare and valuable collection that had belonged to her uncle, Edward Delano, and for the rest of his life, Franklin was absorbed in this hobby.

He was also fascinated by the sea and ships. As a young boy he spent many happy vacations at Fairhaven, Massachusetts, in the treasure-house of sea lore built by his great-grandfather Warren Delano I. The Delano ancestors had always been sailors. During the American Revolution they had built and sailed large vessels. His great-grandfather Delano had owned a fleet of clipper ships that were the fastest of their day. He had made a fortune on the China clipper trade, and Sara's father had followed in the family tradition by making his own fortune in China. Sara often sang sea chanteys and told her son tales of when she was a little girl and had sailed to Hong Kong to join her father.

At Fairhaven the walls were covered with old pictures of ships the family had built, maps, and navigation charts. As a child Franklin loved to sit at the feet of the old sea captain and listen to his tales of the sea. He would climb up into the attic and look through the battered seaman's-chest containing old

sailors'-logs, poring through dusty volumes of wood-
cuts of the whaling fleet. Before he went off to school
at fourteen, Franklin had read and almost knew by
heart a history of the American Navy and the life
of the English hero of Trafalgar, Lord Nelson.

His greatest desire always was to sail. When he
was nine, his father bought a fifty-one-foot sailing
yacht, the *Half Moon*, to sail at Campobello. Franklin was so delighted with the boat he could hardly be
persuaded to leave it, and he would go out with his
father to sail in any kind of weather. When he was
old enough, his mother let him take the *Half Moon*
out with her aboard, and he would sail it while she
read to him. Naval matters became a lifelong interest
that would play an important part in his career.

The boy did not have a formal education in the
usual sense until he entered Groton at fourteen.
However, before he was six, he had learned his
ABC's in English, French, and German. When he was
six years old he had studied for two hours a day with
a German *fräulein*, at the home of his friend Edmund
Rogers. When he was nine he went along with his
family to Bad Nauheim, Germany, and entered a
small local school to improve his knowledge of German language and history. At home that year he was
tutored in French. He spoke it well, and years after-
ward when he was President of the United States he
could still put his knowledge of French to good use.

Franklin always read avidly. He loved such books

as *Little Men, Robinson Crusoe, Swiss Family Robinson*, and Rudyard Kipling's works. He especially enjoyed books about the sea, and liked such magazines as *Scientific American*, which he started reading at nine.

Each day Franklin had a well-ordered routine to follow. He rose at seven, had breakfast at eight, worked on his lessons for two or three hours, and played from noon until one o'clock in the afternoon. After lunch he returned to his studies until four o'clock in the afternoon. Then he had recreation time until dinner. This regulated life was followed through the years until he left for Groton at fourteen.

CHAPTER TWO

★ ★ ★ ★ ★ ★

A DISCIPLINED ADOLESCENCE

In 1896, Franklin was fourteen. He was five feet, three inches tall, with a slender build, lively blue eyes, and a charming smile. He always parted his blond hair neatly in the middle, and he still spoke in a boyish soprano. He was ready to go off to school and eager to start at Groton, one of the most exclusive private academies in the country.

Sara hated to give up her son. She had already kept him home for two years longer than was the custom for one of the Roosevelt's social group. She knew that most boys left home to go to school by the age of twelve, but she could not bear to part with Franklin. When she finally did send him off, she wrote rather poignantly, "It is hard to leave our darling boy. James and I both feel this parting very much."

The Roosevelts had visited Groton for the first time in 1883, a year after Franklin's birth, and had registered their boy. It was logical and fitting that he attend Groton. Ninety per cent of its student body came from families listed in the social register, and most of them went on to Ivy League schools. It was situated in pleasant, rolling Massachusetts country-side, thirty-five miles north of Boston.

The school's founder and long-time headmaster was Endicott Peabody. A boy left Peabody's guidance with the unmistakable stamp of Groton upon him. Peabody was a stern and unbending man who took over the parental authority the boys had left behind. Large, vigorous, with blond hair and an athletic frame, he was thirty-nine the year Franklin entered the school.

For young Franklin, Endicott Peabody became a second father, since his own father was ill and nearing seventy. As a result, the headmaster was a life-long influence. More than anything else, he taught Groton boys determination and courage, characteristics that later enabled Roosevelt to gain the Presidency. When he was President, Roosevelt quoted Peabody's philosophy in an inaugural address and admitted that he had "leaned on the Rector in all these many years far more than most people know."

Peabody stressed concepts of moral and physical vigor, a sense of religious and civic responsibility, and above all, service to church, fellowman, and country. He preached these ideas constantly during

twice-a-day chapel services until the boys accepted
the code as an integral part of their behavior.

Averell Harriman once said of Peabody, "He
would be an awful bully if he weren't such a terrible
Christian." Though the boys feared him, they also
loved him, for he gave his Grotonians a great sense of
personal pride and confidence. It was said that they
had a proud and haughty manner, gazing fixedly two
inches over the head of an acquaintance while talking. Franklin himself was guilty of this habit and had
to work hard to curb it later on as a politician.

As soon as he arrived, Franklin described Groton's campus in a letter home. "The buildings are
built on three sides of a square; the new building,
where we eat, sleep, and study at night, on one side,
the old building, now used as the study and recita-
tions building on the other, and the gymnasium and
fives court between. There are three football fields."
Near the red brick buildings flowed the Nashua
River where the boys rowed, canoed, swam, and
skated.

The boys' living quarters were simple and austere,
for Groton did not believe in pampering its sons.
Franklin lived in a six-by-nine-foot cubicle that contained only a narrow bed, bureau, chair, small rug,
and wall pegs for hanging suits. In his dormitory was
a large common bathroom, and all boys were required to take a cold shower each morning. They

scrubbed up before meals with yellow laundry soap at soapstone sinks and tin basins.

The meals themselves were hardly anything to write home about, though Franklin did, if only to complain in his twice-a-week letter. "We have had sausages or sausage-croquettes for the last three days, but I have managed to keep perfectly well," he wrote.

Classes were called forms in the English manner, with forms I through VI corresponding to the seventh through twelfth grades. Franklin entered the third form, or ninth grade, and was rather at a disadvantage, entering so late, even though his friend Edmund Rogers entered with him, and Franklin's nephew, Taddy, son of his half brother, James Roosevelt Roosevelt, was already a student there. Franklin was eager to jump into activities, but was a bit shy and awkward because he soon found that he was an outsider since friendships had already been formed among the boys.

He had the further handicap of a slight English accent, which he had picked up in his travels abroad, and his manner was perhaps too sophisticated from associating mostly with adults. He also had to contend with the reputation of his nephew, Taddy, nicknamed "Rosy," who was in the fourth form and considered by the others to be a rather strange boy. Everyone made fun of Taddy for being lazy and lacking in school spirit, and when the boys wanted to tease Franklin, they called him Uncle Frank. But Franklin resolutely overlooked this and worked hard to succeed. He wrote home cheerfully, "I am getting on finely both mentally and physically."

He accepted the rigid routine without question. Breakfast was at 7:30, chapel at 8:15, classes from 8:30 until noon. Lunch was followed by afternoon classes and a program of athletics. The boys dressed properly for dinner. This meant a dark suit, white shirt, a stiff collar, and patent leather dress shoes. After dinner there was another chapel service and a study period. Then the boys filed out and shook hands with Rector and Mrs. Peabody. The boys loved the Rector's wife. Generations of Grotonians fondly remembered "Mrs. Peabody's Parlor," an institution where she entertained them and their parents at tea.

The curriculum at the school in 1896 was classical. Latin and Greek were mandatory, and French, German, and English were stressed. Sacred studies, science, and social studies filled out the boys' programs. Curiously, the school neglected study of the United States. The boys learned primarily by rote; creativity and imagination were not stressed. They looked upon courses as obstacles to hurdle. They memorized their material for examinations and then forgot it.

Franklin worked hard on his lessons and did well

in French and German. In October when the first report came out, he stood fourth in a class of nineteen and the Rector wrote, "He strikes me as an intelligent and faithful scholar and a good boy." He was scored high for punctuality and neatness.

Although he had gotten off to a good start, Franklin was not satisfied with being a faithful, punctual, and neat scholar. He wanted to have friends and be a leader. He joined the choir, singing soprano, and played games in Mrs. Peabody's parlor, but he assessed the situation carefully. He saw that the school leaders were the boys on the football and baseball teams. A surefire way to belong, he decided, was to become a star athlete.

Although he was an excellent horseman, a good tennis player, and a skilled sailor, the school heroes did not engage in these sports. They played football. So Franklin went out for the team, even though he had never played the game. He tried hard but was not good enough because of his slight build. He was a bit consoled when he made the "scrub" team, but he did not do well at that either. He soon wrote home requesting a nose guard and then told of whacks, cuts, and bruises and joked about the game: "The only ball I received, I nobly missed, and it landed biff! on my stomach, to the great annoyance of that intricate organ and to the great delight of all present."

Despite the fact he had not made the team, he was an ardent and loyal fan. He wrote in November:

Hurrah, Hurrah, Hurrah
GROTON
46
St. Marks
0
I am hoarse, deaf, and ready to stand on my cocoanut!

When baseball season came, he tried out for that sport and found to his dismay he was even worse. He was relegated to what he called the BBBB team, "Bum Base Ball Boys, the worst players in the school."

The only athletic event in which Franklin excelled was one that required guts and spirit rather than coordination and prowess. That was the high kick, a difficult and painful event. But his obstinacy was finally rewarded. A pan was hung from the ceiling of the gym and each boy tried to kick it as it was gradually raised higher. Franklin persevered and his winning kick was seven feet, three and a half inches. To win he had to land on his neck and left side each time he kicked the pan. He ended up the victor but with his entire left side sore and his left arm swollen.

In the spring he made his first political speech. In a two-minute extemporaneous talk for the debate team, he argued on the subject of the Nicaragua Canal Bill. Later he debated on "Resolved that the U.S. increase the size of the Navy." His six-minute speech won, 27 to 3.

Franklin gradually grew more relaxed. He canoed and played tennis, and even got his first "black mark" for talking in the study room. Probably he set out on purpose to get the mark. He wrote home happily about it, "I am very glad I got it, as I was thought to have no school spirit before."

Discipline at Groton was severe and freely handed out. A boy could receive a black mark for talking or causing distraction in study hall or for any one of a long list of minor offenses. The penalties had to be worked off on Saturday afternoon by copying or doing other chores assigned by a master. A boy who accumulated three or four a term was regarded as a hero.

Six marks, however, led to a dreaded visit to the Rector's study for a severe lecture. An average high-spirited youth might normally accumulate as many as three or four a week, so it was quite a record for Franklin to have avoided a single black mark until the spring term was almost over. After that Franklin caught on to the system. He was more careful to get a few black marks to guarantee his reputation but he never got so many that he had to report to the Rector's study.

A good deal of the discipline at Groton was carried out by upper-form boys with Rector Peabody's blessing. A boy in each dorm was named prefect, and at the top was the senior prefect, the highest position a Groton boy could achieve. They were appointed by the Rector to keep the younger boys in line.

Disciplinary action would take place after evening chapel. The Rector would leave and the senior prefect would ask the whole school to remain seated while he called out a guilty lad's name. The boy had to march out under the eyes of all while sixth-form boys assembled in the senior prefect's study. Out in the corridor they sometimes administered corporal punishment while one of them kept time with a stopwatch to limit the beating the boy might receive.

There were two kinds of severe punishment that held the younger boys in constant fear. These were "boxing" and "pumping." In the basement of the dormitory each boy had a wooden box containing his outdoor boots. If the older boys decided to "box" a boy, they would cram him into his box and shut the lid down tight on him. They kept time with a stopwatch to keep the boy from suffocating. If a boy was "pumped," his head would be forcibly held at the sink and basins of water dumped over him until he felt a sensation of drowning. Franklin, apparently, was resourceful enough never to require such harsh discipline.

Just before that term ended, excitement hit the campus. Franklin's fifth cousin and hero, Theodore Roosevelt, arrived to speak. Franklin was immensely proud of him, especially since he had been appointed the new Assistant Secretary of the Navy after resigning as New York City's Police Commissioner. Teddy made the most of the situation and kept the boys fascinated with his adventures in fighting big-city crime and corruption. After the speech, he invited Franklin to Oyster Bay for the Fourth of July, and Franklin accepted without hesitation.

The crowning day of the year, Prize Day, came in June when Franklin was given his final report, which placed him fourth in his class of seventeen. The Rector rated him very satisfactory. He had failed in Greek but otherwise did well.

After his first year at Groton, he spent a lazy summer sailing and golfing at Campobello Island. By the time fall came he was taller, had gained weight, and his voice had changed. In the fall he dropped choir and took boxing lessons. No longer a new boy, he now had friends and felt that he belonged. His life became a round of studies, football, and golf, and he relaxed so much that he got three or four black marks in one week. He wrote, "I had good fun, quite worth them!"

Ominous talk of Cuba and possible war against Spain began to dominate the news that fall. Franklin followed the events excitedly. After all, his cousin Theodore, as Assistant Secretary of the Navy, was very much involved in the war preparation efforts, making every attempt to build up the Navy. And then Teddy resigned to enter the conflict more directly and was commissioned a lieutenant colonel in the Army.

Franklin wrote thoughtfully of the crisis. "The Spanish situation seems to be unchanged, but I feel that every moment of delay is in the interests of peace, and that the President is doing all he can to prevent war." Young men were rushing into uniform, bands were marching to "Stars and Stripes Forever," and everyone was singing, "There'll Be a Hot Time in the Old Town Tonight."

By spring of 1898 the entire country was aflame with talk of war. In February the U.S.S. *Maine* was blown up in Havana Harbor. Newspapers carried headlines, "Remember the *Maine*," and editorialized about the evils of the Spanish rule. All this stirred up the people and the politicians until President McKinley finally signed the resolution in April that formally declared war on Spain.

Franklin itched to take part in the conflict. He and a close friend, Lathrop Brown, concocted a scheme whereby they might see some wartime fighting. They had heard that the Navy was recruiting men in Boston, and they decided they would enlist.

The boys saved their money to buy rail tickets to Boston. Groton was five miles away from the rail station, so they devised an elaborate plan to sneak away to the station in the local pieman's cart on Sunday. The Saturday night before their enlistment the boys packed in secrecy. The later it got the more they trembled with anticipation. They went to bed but were both shaking with excitement. When morning came, they were hot and flushed and still shaking, but as soon as the prefect saw them, he knew they were ill and not merely excited. He called for the doctor who diagnosed their problem as scarlet fever. The miserable boys were rushed to quarantine in the infirmary, which ended their enlistment plans.

Franklin's mother, in Europe, heard the news of her son's illness. She rushed home, but the doctors would not allow her to enter the quarantined room. With her usual determination, she got around the doctors' orders and entertained her son during his long recuperation period in a most curious manner. She perched high on a ladder outside the window of Franklin's sickroom and read to him through his open window for an hour or so each afternoon.

Franklin went home to Hyde Park early to recuperate, and by June he was well enough to travel to Campobello. That summer Franklin's father gave him his first sailboat, the *New Moon*. It was a twenty-one-foot knockabout with a cabin containing two bunks, and rigged with a mainsail, jib, and spinnaker. Franklin was thrilled. He had often sailed his father's yacht, the *Half Moon*, but she was so big she required a crew. He was a good sailor and familiar with the dangerous tides of the surrounding waters so his parents felt he could manage the smaller *New Moon* alone. Lathrop Brown came up to visit and the two boys practically lived aboard the sailboat. When they were not out navigating the inlets of the bay, they played golf on the nine-hole golf course Franklin had laid out, or swam in an inland lake.

In July during the course of the 115-day Spanish-American War Theodore Roosevelt was in the news again, and the Roosevelts at Campobello followed the news of Teddy's Rough Rider regiment storming the heights of San Juan Hill. He was proclaimed a hero and everyone urged him to come home to New York and run for governor of the state.

Soon after Frankin returned to Groton for the fifth form, Teddy Roosevelt entered the New York gubernatorial campaign. Franklin's father, a lifelong Democrat, bolted his party to promote his cousin's Republican candidacy. The Hyde Park and Oyster Bay Roosevelts joined in helping Teddy carry the state by 25,000 votes. Franklin and his friends at Groton went wild when they heard the news. Franklin returned to Hyde Park and journeyed to Albany with his parents for Teddy's inauguration.

Franklin's idol, the new governor of New York, returned to Groton soon after his election and spoke to the boys on the importance of men of ability seeking public office. "If a man has courage, goodness, and brains no limit can be placed to the greatness of the work he may accomplish. He is the man needed today in politics," Teddy told his admiring audience.

Franklin listened thoughtfully to his cousin's advice. He was beginning to mature. He had to see football games, enter golf tournaments, and attend faculty-student suppers. But he also began to think about more important matters, such as his future.

For one thing, he noticed that girls could be fun. He made plans for a Christmas party at Hyde Park, asking his parents to find "some decent partner" for him so he would not "get palmed off on some ice-cart" of a girl. Curiously, he wrote, "How about Teddy Robinson and Eleanor Roosevelt? They would go well and help to fill out chinks."

For the first time he began to show an interest in helping less fortunate people, a trait that would someday earn him the respect and gratitude of America. He turned some of his interests toward religion and charitable work. He joined the Missionary Society, which helped the Boston Boys' Club run a summer camp for underprivileged boys. He took on a job as special visitor to a nearby elderly lady. He visited her twice a week to see that she had coal and water, fed her chickens, and helped dig her home out of snowstorms.

During his sixth form he became a dormitory prefect, which was not quite as great a distinction as it sounded since over half his class had a turn before the year's end. He was conscientious at the job, though, and helped keep his thirty-six charges in good order.

It was a successful year for Franklin, though distressing news of his father's increasing illnesses upset him periodically. His father was better by Christmas and Franklin embarked upon a round of parties, theater, and dances. Easter came, and he found he had to wear eyeglasses along with braces on his teeth. He took it all in his stride and ordered spectacles and a pair of pince-nez. That term he was baseball team manager and worked hard rolling the diamond, keeping the equipment in good shape, and accompanying the team on trips. He could not be a star, but he was faithful to the team, and his loyalty never wavered. That year Groton beat St. Marks, 7–6.

Franklin sadly watched June, 1900, arrive. "As the end of school approaches we the departing form are feeling very blue," he wrote. By graduation week he was in good spirits again. "The strife is o'er, the battle won! What a joyful yet sad day this has been," he wrote home. His final report card showed a respectable B average, and Mr. Peabody wrote, "He has been a thoroughly faithful scholar & a most satisfactory member of this school throughout his course. I part with Franklin with reluctance."

His peers at Groton had differing opinions about Franklin and his character. The younger boys described him as self-possessed, intelligent, with a friendly and understanding smile. The sixth-formers were a bit more critical. One said he had an independent and cocky attitude and was argumentative and sarcastic. It was true Franklin always enjoyed arguing and tended to take the opposing viewpoint to bait the other fellows.

His father was too ill in June to attend commencement but he and Sara were pleased when their son won the Latin Prize and received a forty-volume set of Shakespeare as a reward.

Armed with Latin verbs and Shakespearean drama, the tall, gangling youth set off for college. He always retained fond memories of the school, and forty years later he wrote admiringly to the Rector, "I count it among the blessings of my life that it was given to me in formative years to have the privilege of your guiding hand."

CHAPTER THREE

★ ★ ★ ★ ★ ★

MATURING YEARS AT HARVARD

At eighteen Franklin stood on the threshold of the twentieth century, not knowing where he was headed but eager to proceed. He left Hyde Park for Harvard University ready to absorb the life of Cambridge and Boston, called by admirers the Athens of America and the Hub of the Universe.

Franklin, though tall and awkward looking, was in reality a charming and self-confident young man as he left for college. He had not wanted to attend Harvard. All his life he had dreamed of going to the U.S. Naval Academy at Annapolis to fulfill his childhood wish of becoming a midshipman. But his father objected to his dream of a Navy career, strongly urging that his son follow in his own footsteps and earn a law degree. So Franklin deferred to his father's wishes and joined the ranks of other Groton classmates who were off to Harvard in 1900.

He and Lathrop Brown decided to room together at college and took an elegant three-room suite at

Westmorly Court, located on Harvard's "Gold Coast." This was an area of expensive dwellings along Mt. Auburn Street where exclusive clubs and dormitories were located. Wealthy students lived on the Gold Coast, and Franklin happily joined his peers.

After settling down at Westmorly Court, he assumed the familiar prep-school pattern of eating at the private Groton table in Cambridge and gathering for an evening of small talk at nearby Sanborn's billiard parlor. Most of the fellows from Groton, St. Marks, St. Pauls, and Pomfret went there, Franklin wrote.

The circumscribed life of the young men on the Gold Coast was a world apart from other students. Across the avenue in the Yard, decrepit and uncomfortable buildings housed many other students whose family background or financial condition made them social outsiders to the Gold Coasters. Endicott Peabody, official minister to the university, often spoke out against the gap between Mt. Auburn Street and the Yard, for the two groups had little contact and few opportunities to mingle. Campus life was controlled by the wealthy students from the more prominent schools and families.

The university offered an excellent atmosphere in which to learn. Its president, Charles W. Eliot, embarking upon his fourth decade of leadership, had introduced various reforms such as an elective system of courses for the students and voluntary attendance at classes and had gathered an impressive group of men to teach the 1,750 boys enrolled in 1900.

A few hours after arriving, Franklin sat down to write his parents, "Here I am, in Cambridge and in twelve hours I shall be a fully registered member of the Class of 1904." He immediately consulted with his adviser about courses. He avoided the easy and popular classes and took the maximum number of subjects. He had anticipated some of the Harvard requirements at Groton and was able to complete the required work on a bachelor's degree in three years.

The *Harvard Alumni Bulletin* commented on his program, "Judged by football standards . . . [it] was anything but a snap." He took history of English literature, survey of European history, French prose and poetry, American government, Latin, and geology. His teachers were some of Harvard's outstanding professors. Over the years Franklin did passably well, maintaining a C average in his courses.

That he received passing grades was astonishing, considering the heavy extracurricular program and demanding social schedule he kept. But he had energy and was able to work hard enough to pass courses without letting them interfere with his many other activities.

The social relationship between Boston and the university was a close one at the time. Beacon Hill hostesses relied heavily on Cambridge to supply

young men for their society events, and they immediately placed Franklin on their lists as an eligible
young man for a whirl of social affairs. He adapted
easily to the genteel society of Boston since it was
much the same as Hyde Park. His social life was
filled with dinner engagements, social calls, the
theater, and parties. "My dress-suit looked like a
dream and was much admired," he wrote, and "don't
forget the double-breasted coat," he reminded his
mother.

Franklin decided to try out for athletics but,
though he made a valiant attempt, his light physique
and lack of real athletic ability prohibited much success. He was six feet, one and a half inches tall, but
weighed only one hundred and forty-six pounds and
found he was not powerful enough for the freshman
football squad, though he did make the scrubs. He
also tried out for crew but could manage only as
stroke on an intramural team and did little rowing in
college except on an alumni crew against the Groton
varsity in 1904. Unfortunately, his old grads lost.

Franklin faced the obvious fact that he would be
no campus athletic hero, so he turned his energies in
other directions and found he did have talent for
winning office. He was the only freshman elected
captain of a scrub team, captain of the third crew of
the Newell Boating Club, and secretary of the Freshman Glee Club that year.

From the first he was happy at Harvard. He found

he fit in easily and by the year's end had assumed all
the characteristics and activities of a typical colle-
gian. He sent home for a pipe, spent weekends duck
shooting with new friends, attended football games,
and even found enough time to continue his Groton
work with the Boys' Club in Boston, teaching underprivileged boys and participating in their sports
programs. He remained close to Groton and returned for frequent visits.

That fall he got involved in the Presidential campaign since his cousin Teddy was running for Vice-
President on the Republican ticket. Franklin joined
the campus Republican Club and in a letter home
described a torchlight parade in which he marched.
"We wore red caps and gowns & marched by classes
into Boston & thro' all the principal streets, about 8
miles in all. The crowds to see it were huge all along
the route & we were dead tired at the end."

He also wrote home that he was trying out for the
Harvard Crimson, the daily newspaper, and that "if I
work hard for two years I may be made an editor,"
he said. He competed with sixty-eight candidates
who also coveted positions, but Franklin worked
hard and by spring was often putting in six hours a
day on assignments for the paper. He got his lucky
break when Theodore Roosevelt unwittingly gave
him a major scoop.

After Teddy was elected Vice-President of the
United States, he arrived at Cambridge for a speak-

ing engagement. When Franklin called him to arrange a visit, Teddy replied, "I'll see you when I come out to lecture. I'm speaking for Professor Lowell, in Government One." Franklin knew he had an inside story and rushed with the scoop to the *Crimson*, which featured the news on page one. As a result the class was so jammed with onlookers there was hardly room for the regular students. This annoyed Professor Lowell, but impressed the *Crimson* board, which elected Franklin one of five new associate editors in June.

During his first year at Harvard, Franklin achieved some of the recognition he had been waiting for, but he was sorry his father could not witness his triumph. Earlier that year his father's health had grown worse. Franklin's letters home showed increasing concern for his father's heart condition. He often made a special trip home to be with his parents. He encouraged his mother to take his father to Aiken, South Carolina, where she had rented a house hoping that the warm climate might soothe her husband. However, James Roosevelt had several heart attacks that autumn, and in November was taken to New York City and put under the constant supervision of the family doctor.

On December 3 Franklin wrote his last letter addressed to "My dearest Mama and Papa." A few days later he received a telegram summoning him to the apartment in New York City. Franklin, his mother, and half brother James were present when James Roosevelt died on December 8, 1900.

The family remained at Hyde Park until the new year when Franklin returned to school. His mother was a widow at the age of forty-six and desolate, but she tried to struggle through the winter alone at Hyde Park. However, she found it too lonely and for the next two winters rented an apartment in Boston to be nearer her son. Franklin visited his mother often and during the winters of 1902 and 1903 sometimes held parties in her apartment.

The summer after his father's death, he encouraged his mother to travel on the Continent with him and some friends. They cruised the fjords of Norway and visited Germany, Switzerland, and France. While in Paris they learned the shocking news of the attempted assassination of President McKinley. They rushed home and, twelve days later when they landed in New York, they heard that the shooting had been fatal. Franklin's cousin Theodore Roosevelt had become the twenty-sixth President of the United States.

In spite of Franklin's keen interest in his cousin's work in Washington, he took a heavy load of course work his second year, including economics, American history, constitutional and political history, English parliamentary history, paleontology, English composition, and public speaking. He spent long hours of work on the *Crimson* and was appointed to represent the newspaper at the Yale University Bicentennial. This was a particularly unusual moment in history. President Theodore Roosevelt was joined on the speaker's platform by two future Presidents. One was the dignified and impressive President of Princeton, Woodrow Wilson. The other was an awkward young Harvard reporter, Franklin Roosevelt.

Christmas was a carefree holiday. He sailed on the Hudson in a new iceboat and hosted a party at Hyde Park. After the holidays he went to Alice Roosevelt's debut in Washington, a gala ball at the White House. "The dance was great fun, & something to be always remembered," he wrote his mother.

Since the new President in the White House was busily involved in trust-busting, Franklin found his cousin increasingly unpopular with the wealthy families of his friends at Harvard. He had defended Teddy frequently that fall, and this did not make him popular with his associates. Some even began to call him a radical. The reputation may have caused the unhappiness that followed in January when time came for sophomore club hazing. Franklin had looked forward confidently to the ritual. "I am about to be slaughtered, but quite happy, nevertheless," he wrote his mother. "The Agony will last till Wednesday night . . ."

He was certain of final membership in some club because of his background and was elected to the Institute of 1770 and D.K.E. He was also tapped for

Alpha Delta Phi, the Fly Club. His great disappointment, however, was in being passed over by the highest-ranking of all the clubs, Porcellian, which his cousin Theodore had joined. This was a blow that he later called one of the most bitter moments of his life.

However, Franklin was developing the ability to ignore defeat and build on his successes. He turned his attention to participating in his clubs and became head librarian of the Fly Club in his junior year, was elected to the library committee of the new Harvard Union, and became librarian of the Hasty Pudding Club. As librarian for these organizations he began wandering through secondhand bookshops in Boston to buy books, talking with shop owners and browsing among the dusty shelves. Soon he was not only buying books for the libraries but adding to his own private collection.

Books on American life absorbed him and he decided to narrow his interest in collecting to the Navy, his childhood fascination. With his spare money he bought all the books, pamphlets, manuscripts, articles, and prints he could find on his specialty until he had a noteworthy collection. He also gathered books about the Hudson Valley, children's literature, and miniature books. Book collecting brought him great satisfaction, and he pursued the hobby throughout his life and was still collecting a few months before his death.

By the end of his junior year Franklin had completed all the course requirements for his degree, but he had no intention of leaving Harvard for another year, for he had won the coveted post of editor in chief of the *Crimson*. He had gained status as a campus leader and returned in September with abundant plans for editing the paper. He took graduate courses in history, economics, and English but with no real thought of working on a master's degree.

He reveled in his campus leadership and worked diligently to put out the weekly newspaper. He took his editorship seriously and throughout the next half year wrote stirring editorials on subjects typical of college newspapers. Frequently he heckled the football team and exhorted it on to greater victory or complained about lack of school spirit and weak cheering sections. As a matter of fact, his editorials became so strident that he received complaints from the readers about his excessive sarcasm and had to tone down his ardor. He even wrote one serious piece on the "splendid triumphs" of the Harvard chess team.

He showed little interest in matters outside the university but did editorialize on inadequate fire protection in the dormitories and persuaded university officials to install more extinguishers, hydrants, and ladders. He did little to improve the quality of the paper, but the *Harvard Alumni Bulletin* assessed him as "at least mildly distinguished for the animation of his many editorials, and for certain college reforms which he engineered."

Franklin's term as editor brought him into contact with a broader spectrum of the student body than he would have encountered otherwise. Perhaps this further stimulated his sympathy and understanding for groups other than his own. He wrote an indignant editorial calling for reforms to make election procedures more democratic, condemning the fact that boys who were not members of the elite clubs could not hope to win a student body office. "There is a higher duty than to vote for one's personal friends and that is to secure for the whole class leaders who really deserve the position," he wrote.

He himself was one of six nominees for marshal of the senior class in the 1903–4 election. He lost but was later elected to permanent chairmanship of his Class Committee.

The winter of 1903–4 was strenuous for young Roosevelt, for not only was he writing editorials and completing his courses, but he was courting the girl he wanted to marry.

Many times through the years he had associated with Eleanor Roosevelt, his godfather's daughter and a distant cousin. They had played together as children, but he had not seen her for several years until he met her one day on a train bound for Hyde Park. She was eighteen and not strikingly beautiful. But she was tall and willowy, with lovely fair hair and blue eyes. He had a pleasant conversation with her on the train, then saw her again later and once more was taken by her lively spirit, perceptive mind, and radiant warmth.

It did not hurt either that she was a niece of his idol, the President of the United States. He began to see her whenever he could, traveling to New York to meet her. Eleanor was already interested in the poor and their social problems and worked at a settlement house in the slums of New York. There she taught courses in dancing and calisthenics to the neighborhood children. She worked with the Consumers' League investigating scandalous conditions of working girls in dress factories and department stores. Sometimes Franklin met her at the settlement house to escort her home, and one time he visited a slum dwelling in one of the East Side's worst tenement houses. He was horrified at what he saw.

By the time he was a junior at Harvard, Franklin knew he had found the girl he wanted to marry, and Eleanor was equally sure that she had found in Franklin someone to give her the security she had always lacked. Though she had grown up just a few miles from Franklin's Hyde Park home, she had not shared his childhood. Eleanor had suffered through a lonely and unhappy existence. Her mother, Anna Hall, had been one of the most beautiful and popular of the debutantes of her day, and all three of Eleanor's aunts were also great beauties. It was Eleanor's misfortune to be a solemn and awkward child. She was called an ugly duckling by her aunts, and her own mother called her Granny because of her serious nature.

Eleanor adored her handsome father, and he fondly called her his little Nell or Golden Hair. But tragedy struck the family, and by the time Eleanor was ten both her parents were dead. She was handed over to her Grandmother Hall, who reared her sternly, as if to compensate for the failures she had endured in the upbringing of her own children, Eleanor's aunts and uncles.

Occasionally during these years of childhood Eleanor saw Franklin at family gatherings, and at one Christmas party when she was at her most awkward adolescent stage, she felt terribly grateful when he asked her to dance.

When she was fifteen, her grandmother decided to send her abroad to complete her education. She went to Mlle. Souvestre, who taught in England, and for three years Eleanor flourished under the skillful guidance of the headmistress. When she had to return home at eighteen to face the ordeal of coming out into society, she was miserable once again. She wanted to go to college, but Grandmother Hall vetoed the idea, so Eleanor returned unhappily to the somber atmosphere of Tivoli, the Hall country home.

However, Eleanor had unusual spunk. She took an

interest in her younger brother, "Hall," and saw to it that he was sent to Groton where she visited him once each term. She finally persuaded her grandmother to permit her to leave Tivoli and move into New York City to live with her cousins, Mr. and Mrs. Henry Parish, Jr., a more stable family than the Halls. This move finally gave her some freedom, and she began to come out of her shell, to feel more secure, and to pursue her goal of working with the poor and downtrodden.

About that time she met Franklin again and began to join the groups of young people that Franklin gathered together for parties at home and in Boston. She had always been shy around boys, and at her own coming-out party, only one young man had asked her to dance. It was natural that a charming, self-assured, and handsome fellow like Franklin would have left her dazzled. They spent quiet times getting to know each other, always under the watchful eyes of a chaperone, the custom of the time. Eleanor went to Campobello for a visit during the summer, bringing along her personal maid as chaperone.

By the end of Franklin's junior year, when Eleanor was nineteen and Franklin twenty-two, he asked her to marry him. Franklin broke the news in December, 1903, to his shocked mother, who could only write in her diary, "Franklin gave me quite a startling announcement." The news surprised and disappointed her.

He had written: "Dearest Mama, I know what pain I must have caused you and you know I wouldn't do it if I really could have helped it . . . I know my own mind, have known it for a long time, and know that I could never think otherwise: Result: I am the happiest man just now in the world; likewise the luckiest—And for you, dear Mummy, you know that nothing can ever change what we have always been & always will be to each other—only now you have two children to love & to love you— and Eleanor as you know will always be a daughter to you in every true way. . . ."

Eleanor also tried in her shy way to reassure her future mother-in-law. "Dearest Cousin Sally," she wrote at about the same time, "I must write you & thank you for being so good to me yesterday. I know just how you feel & how hard it must be, but I do so want you to learn to love me a little. You must know that I will always try to do what you wish for I have grown to love you very dearly during the past summer. . . . Always devotedly, Eleanor."

But Sara Roosevelt was unhappy about the marriage. She had laid careful plans for her son's return to Hyde Park after graduation, so that she would have his companionship once more. She did not object to Eleanor herself, for the girl was precisely the kind she would have chosen for her son eventually. But she firmly felt that her son was much too young, had not yet made a place for himself in the world, and had little to offer a woman.

She did everything in her power to dissuade him, even using the delaying tactic of planning a Caribbean cruise for that spring. Franklin consented and set out with her and Lathrop Brown on a relaxing six-week tour. He enjoyed himself, but he did not forget his fiancée as his mother had hoped he would. She tried to pursuade the Ambassador to England to hire Franklin as his secretary, but that scheme failed too. She did convince the couple to delay any public announcement of the engagement for a year. But finally, when all tactics proved unsuccessful, Sara decided she had better submit gracefully. She set out to do precisely what her son had suggested, looking upon Eleanor as another child, a daughter, to manage and plan for. The struggle had really only begun.

Harvard commencement came in June, 1904. Sara and Eleanor attended and watched proudly as Franklin sat upon the platform as a class officer. Later Sara commented, "His father and I always expected a great deal of Franklin. We thought he ought to take prizes, and we were pleased but not surprised when he did. After all he had many advantages that other boys did not have."

After the Harvard ceremony, Franklin visited Groton to celebrate the Twentieth Prize Day, which may have meant more to him than his own college graduation. President Theodore Roosevelt was the featured speaker, and Franklin took to heart the advice of the President. "Much has been given you; therefore, we have a right to expect much from you." Franklin felt he could live up to the President's words.

CHAPTER FOUR
★★★★★

MARRIAGE AND POLITICS

During the fall of 1904, Franklin settled down in New York City. He entered Columbia University Law School, which he had chosen in order to be near his fiancée, Eleanor. They were to be married in the spring. That November he voted for the first time in a national election, casting his ballot for a Roosevelt for President. Theodore ran on the Republican ticket, and Franklin said later, "I thought he was a better Democrat than the Democratic candidate."

Franklin attended law classes faithfully and did the necessary studying, but his impending marriage occupied much of his thoughts while a well-filled social schedule occupied his spare time. Studying law was understandably dull. He always made certain his academic record was sufficient to pass, but he had little interest beyond that.

He purchased a suitable engagement ring for Eleanor, and prepared an official announcement of the wedding, to be held in March. It was to be a grand society affair, of course, but the planning was more complicated than an ordinary wedding since Eleanor's uncle Theodore, the President of the United States, had consented to give away his favorite niece in marriage. Complex arrangements had to be made for the President's presence and safety.

Less than two weeks before the wedding Theodore was inaugurated as President. Franklin and Eleanor attended the inaugural ceremonies in Washington, witnessing the impressive spectacle with the immediate family just behind the President on the Capitol steps. Young Franklin Roosevelt in his wildest dreams hoped someday to follow his cousin to those same steps. That dramatic moment must have given him a faint glimmer of hope.

They rushed back to New York and excitedly awaited March 17, their wedding day, which fell on St. Patrick's Day. In effect, President Roosevelt had actually chosen the wedding day since he planned to review a St. Patrick's Day parade in New York City that day and the date was set to accommodate his New York trip. The date incidentally had sentimental significance for Eleanor since it was her mother's birthday. The wedding took place in the adjoining homes of Eleanor's cousin Mrs. Parish and Mrs. Parish's mother, near Fifth Avenue. Sliding doors between the two homes opened to allow room for the many invited guests.

On the day of the wedding huge crowds milled

around the house, and seventy policemen were assigned to keep people away from the President. The
traffic jam was monumental. Though the police tried
to keep a path open, many invited guests could not
push their way through until after the ceremony.
Nearby a band blared "The Wearin' of the Green,"
almost drowning out the sound of the wedding
march.

Despite all the commotion, the ceremony was not
interrupted. Eleanor was tall and slender in a heavy
white satin gown with a long train and veil of an-
tique lace. She was led in by the President. Lathrop
Brown was Franklin's best man, and Teddy's daughter, Alice, was maid of honor. Franklin was almost
late for his own wedding. He, Brown, and Reverend
Peabody, who performed the ceremony, were so
deep in conversation while waiting for the wedding
to begin that they did not realize the procession was
under way until after the music had actually started.
They caught themselves at the critical moment and
made it to the altar in time.

As Reverend Peabody began to read the ceremony,
crowds outside cried, "We want Teddy," and the
guests had to strain to catch the words. The young
couple must have felt the tenseness of having such
an illustrious member of their wedding party.
Shortly after the ceremony, Teddy adjourned into
the library of the adjoining house, and the guests
naturally followed him. The bride and groom sud-

S 3

denly realized they stood alone in the receiving line, so they followed their friends and stood on the edge of the crowd listening to the President tell an amusing story.

The newlyweds left for a short honeymoon at Hyde Park. They postponed a real honeymoon until the summer, when Franklin would be free from studying. Then they explored Europe leisurely, touring Italy, the Alps, Germany, Paris, London, and rural England and Scotland, where they had relatives.

It was a perfect honeymoon, filled with treasured memories of cathedrals and museums, poking around bookshops to buy rare books and prints, collecting furniture, linens, and clothes, and in Scotland purchasing the first of many Scotty dogs. Along the way, the honeymooners received a good deal more attention than ordinary tourists because of their Presidential connections. In London they actually found themselves installed in the royal suite of the most fashionable hotel, the cost far beyond what they expected to pay. "President Roosevelt and Bride on Honeymoon," read the mistaken caption of an English newspaper.

The return voyage was a miserable one for Eleanor. She suffered from more seasickness than usual, probably because she was in the first months of pregnancy. Upon arriving in New York City, the young couple set up housekeeping at 125 East 36th

Street, a house that Franklin's mother had rented for them. Except for wedding presents and a few European objects, Eleanor had nothing to do with furnishing the house. Sara Roosevelt made all the decisions about decorating and furnishing and even hiring the servants. With some reluctance Eleanor submitted to her mother-in-law's wishes, since she was shy and insecure in those early years of marriage.

Sara then decided to present the newlyweds with a special gift. She drew a sketch of a house and wrote, "A Christmas present to Franklin & Eleanor from Mama—Number & street not yet quite decided." Franklin was delighted and plunged into detailed planning with his mother for a four-story brick house with an identical house adjoining for his mother.

Eleanor was not consulted, and her opinion was not sought on the plans for the new house. One evening, shortly after the couple had moved into their new home, Eleanor sat before her new dressing table in front of her husband and suddenly burst into violent sobbing. Franklin, bewildered, asked why she was crying. She sobbed that she did not like to live in a house that was not hers in any way, one that she had done nothing about and that did not represent the way she wanted to live. Franklin managed to comfort his tearful wife, but he did not seem to understand her emotional outburst. He never seemed to resent his mother's intrusion in their lives.

Eleanor managed to hold her emotions in check

and became a dutiful, loving, obedient daughter-in-law and wife. After all, Franklin's mother held most of the purse strings. When Franklin's father had died, Franklin's share of the estate was left in trust and his mother was his sole guardian. Most of the estate was left to her outright. Sara's father had also given her a large inheritance, making her a wealthy woman.

Franklin's share of the estate gave them an income of about $5,000 a year, and this, combined with Eleanor's inheritance, provided them about $12,000 yearly. This was ample, but emergencies constantly arose, and Sara was always generous and free with her checkbook.

Franklin was still in law school at Columbia, beginning his second year after returning from his European honeymoon. In the spring of his third year he passed the New York State bar examinations, allowing him to enter practice without further study. He did not even bother to complete his university courses and never received his law degree.

During the next ten years Franklin and Eleanor's family life settled into a pattern. Franklin took a law position and then pursued an incipient career in politics and government. Eleanor had six children in that ten-year period. Anna Eleanor was the oldest, born May 3, 1906. She was followed by five boys. James was born December 23, 1907; Franklin Delano, Jr., born March 18, 1909, died eight months later; Elliott, September 23, 1910; another Franklin Delano, Jr., August 17, 1914; and John Aspinwall, March 13, 1916.

During those years Eleanor was completely absorbed with the duties of new motherhood, baby care, and household management, with a retinue of nurses and servants. Her mother-in-law guided her in most of her decisions. It was not until years later when Eleanor had grown more mature and had acquired a greater measure of self-confidence and assertiveness that she could gradually assume independence from the strong-willed Sara Roosevelt.

After Franklin had successfully passed the state bar examination in 1907, he went to work for the distinguished New York law firm of Carter, Ledyard and Milburn, the trustees for J. P. Morgan. Though a junior clerk in the firm, he gained some legal experience as head clerk in charge of municipal court cases and the firm's admiralty division. He learned much about judicial procedure in minor courts and how to handle witnesses, but he soon realized he was not completely absorbed by this career. He was marking time, working in the firm until an opportunity might present itself that would really absorb his total energies.

In his usual ebullient way, Roosevelt threw himself into civic activities in Hyde Park and club memberships in the city. Like his father, Franklin was respected in the small community of Hyde Park. The handsome and energetic young lawyer soon was approached by the town's political leaders. His vitality had caught their eye, and they shrewdly figured he might be a vote-getter. After all, he possessed not only the magic name of Roosevelt but also the necessary money to put into a campaign. In 1910 the political bosses needed a Democratic nominee for state senator, and they had nothing to lose in choosing a political unknown since the senate seat was traditionally Republican. The local Democratic chief called on Roosevelt and asked him to drop by headquarters in Poughkeepsie.

Roosevelt did just that, casually arriving one day dressed in riding clothes. This was hardly what the startled politicians expected. They took one look at the dapper young man and said, "If you run, you'll have to take off those yellow boots and put on pants."

It was the chance Roosevelt had waited for. He took off his boots, rolled up his sleeves, and got a brainstorm. He decided to use an automobile to campaign in and hired a fire-engine-red Maxwell roadster to travel across the district. Roosevelt proceeded to give every citizen the opportunity to know him by sight; he spoke in every town and village and at any corner where a potential voter would listen. Nobody had ever campaigned in the state by automobile before. He kept on the move, speaking tirelessly from the back of the open car, and on one occasion overshot the New York State line and found himself campaigning before a bewildered crowd in Connecticut.

Roosevelt chose to base his campaign on a call for clean government and an attack on the corrupt practices of the political machine bosses. When he accepted the nomination, he maintained his "absolute independence" from any party faction or machine.

When election day came in November the Republicans were astounded. The Democratic upstart candidate for state senator won and became the second Democrat to hold the seat from that district since 1856, the only other winner being in 1888. The decision was close; he won by only 1,140 votes.

Roosevelt had his big chance. He had no intention of serving out his term in Albany as the traditionally silent freshman senator. He had hardly settled in Albany and warmed his senate chair when he audaciously jumped into a bitter political battle against the bosses that captured the headlines of newspapers and caught the eye of politicians across the state.

To political experts, Roosevelt's fight no doubt seemed foolhardy. Roosevelt, a political novice, took on the mighty Tammany Hall machine, whose power in Democratic politics in New York State was massive and total. Early in 1911, the boss of Tammany had handpicked William F. ("Blue-Eyed Billy") Sheehan to fill the U.S. Senate vacancy. Federal senators were chosen in state legislatures at that time, so

the Tammany machine believed the election of Sheehan was a simple matter. However, they did not
reckon with the newcomer in the senate with a stubborn Dutch chin and an iron determination to win.

Roosevelt gathered his forces for the fray, and
managed to round up a group of reform-minded
Democrats who wanted to defeat the entrenched
machine. Their tactic was to bolt the caucus that
would vote on Sheehan, thus losing a majority vote
for the Tammany choice. The bosses were enraged at
the political shenanigans of this newcomer from upstate. But this was the beginning of a dramatic ten-
week deadlock between the Roosevelt reformers and
the Tammany machine, and all legislative business
came to a standstill as the machine fought to beat
the young politician.

During the next two and a half months and
through sixty-four ballots Roosevelt showed the political genius and determination of his later years as
he maneuvered to choose another candidate for U.S.
Senator. His reform group was just about ready to
throw in the towel when Sheehan finally withdrew
his candidacy in favor of a compromise candidate.
Roosevelt's political courage and dramatic sense of
timing had barely won the day, and he exulted in his
first major political victory within the party.

People talked about the "second Roosevelt," the
tall, lithe, hard-working state senator who had
caused murmurs in the Tammany machine with his

comment reported in *The New York Times*, "There is nothing I love so much as a good fight."

He worked hard as senator, learning about the state's conservation problems as chairman of the Forest, Fish, and Game Committee, and he came out against the utilities lobby and in favor of farm relief. Through the Roosevelt home in Albany passed a steady stream of political acquaintances, and the new legislator became friends with such men as Robert F. Wagner, Al Smith, and a man who would serve the rest of his lifetime with Roosevelt, Louis McHenry Howe.

In 1912 Roosevelt ran again. His campaign was based primarily on agrarian progressivism, bipartisanship, anti-bossism, and the needs of his constituents. Midway through the battle, however, he was stricken with typhoid and was forced out of action. Instead of giving up, he called upon Louis Howe to run his campaign. Howe was an Albany correspondent for the New York *Herald*. He was a small, ugly, untidy man whose only real interest was political maneuvering. In the tall, handsome, and debonair Roosevelt, Howe saw a bright political future, perhaps even the Presidency of the United States. From that moment on, he stayed close to Franklin Roosevelt and guided much of Roosevelt's political destiny.

With Howe at the helm in his bid for a second state senatorial term, Roosevelt won with a handy majority. Things looked fine for the young politician in New York State, but bigger events were destined to follow in quick succession; these would move him into the arena of national politics before he could complete his second term.

Roosevelt had gone to Baltimore in June, 1912, to attend the Democratic convention that would ultimately nominate Woodrow Wilson for President. Roosevelt was not a delegate to the convention, but he nevertheless organized a group of eager young college men and set out to contact every delegate he could reach on behalf of Wilson, whom he deeply admired. The convention was a wild affair. Wilson started out with only a slim chance of winning the nomination, but on the forty-sixth ballot he finally emerged the victor.

The jubilant Roosevelt wired home, "Wilson nominated this afternoon all my plans vague splendid triumph." Roosevelt had formed several important friendships during the convention that would prove influential to his career. Among them were William G. McAdoo, Joseph E. Davies, Henry Morgenthau, Sr., and Josephus Daniels.

After Woodrow Wilson won the election and became President of the United States, one of his early appointments was Josephus Daniels for Secretary of the Navy. Daniels remembered the loyal Wilson worker in Baltimore to whom he had taken an instant liking, and he proposed Roosevelt's name to the

President for the job of Assistant Secretary of the Navy in the new administration.

Daniels approached FDR about the job and asked, "Would you like to be Assistant Secretary?" Roosevelt's reply was immediate. "How would I like it? I'd like it bully well!"

So the young legislator, no doubt feeling that destiny must have willed it, proudly followed in the footsteps of his illustrious cousin. A second Roosevelt became Assistant Secretary of the Navy. He was just a little over thirty years old and thus became the youngest man to hold the post in Navy history.

CHAPTER FIVE

★ ★ ★ ★ ★ ★

LEADERSHIP AT THE NAVY

When Secretary of the Navy Josephus Daniels consulted the Republican senator from New York, Elihu Root, about choosing young Franklin Roosevelt as his assistant, the senator thought for a moment. Then he advised the Secretary somewhat tartly, "You know the Roosevelts, don't you? Whenever a Roosevelt rides, he wishes to ride in front." Daniels nevertheless chose Roosevelt, but he had ample occasion to remember the caustic comment in the seven and a half years Roosevelt served him.

FDR was sworn in as Assistant Secretary of the Navy on his eighth wedding anniversary, March 17, 1913. That evening he sat down and wrote:

Dearest Mama
I am baptized, confirmed, sworn in, vaccinated—and somewhat at sea! For over an hour I have been signing papers which had to be accepted on faith—but I hope luck will keep me out of jail.
All well, but I will have to work like a new tur-

*bine to master this job—but it will be done even if
it takes all summer.*

*Your affec. son
Franklin D. Roosevelt*

The Roosevelts settled temporarily in Washington, D.C., in their Aunty Bye's house on N Street, which they had visited frequently. They searched and found a larger home at 2131 R Street that would accommodate their growing family, and for the next seven years Roosevelt worked at a job that gave him vast experience in governmental affairs and paved the way to future success as the nation's leader.

He was young, brash, and impetuous. He was a builder with a positive gift for organizing and arranging a smoothly running operation, and he had the opportunity to develop this talent in the Navy. He immediately assumed a leadership role in the department. Without reservation he advocated a big Navy, capable of protecting the country. Roosevelt had already perceived the ominous signs that indicated America's involvement in a worldwide conflict. When he took on the new job, he committed himself to a Navy second to none and proclaimed these convictions openly.

In 1913, during an era when government was still a comparatively small operation, the assistant's job was already one of huge management responsibilities. The Navy had far-flung operations, which included not only maintaining a large fleet but also employing many civilians in Navy yards and installations. The assistant secretary's particular responsibilities centered around civilian personnel operations, balancing delicate relations between military and civilian officials, and handling the budget. The dynamic young FDR was not content to stick to his particular duties. He purposefully involved himself in as many operations as possible, losing no chance to advance his knowledge of the Navy and expand his own sphere of influence. He rapidly mastered the intricacies of his job, and he showed irritation and impatience with Secretary Daniels, who did not move ahead quickly enough to suit the impatient young assistant secretary.

Roosevelt ran everywhere, meeting public officials, probing labor contracts, conversing with admirals. These many contacts enabled him to gain extensive knowledge of the Navy. "Young Roosevelt is very promising, but I should think he'd wear himself out on the promiscuous and extended contacts he maintains with people," Secretary of War Newton Baker said later. But it was from this wide assortment of men ranging from machinists and labor union officials to foreign diplomats and the President himself that Roosevelt absorbed ideas.

One of his first realizations was the importance of the admirals, and he set out to cultivate the respect and confidence of this group. They soon recognized that unlike the unsympathetic and puritanical Daniels, Roosevelt was a dashing and spirited man who loved the sea, knew nautical terms, and most important had a philosophy of "big Navy" in complete accordance with theirs. They turned to him for leadership, hoping he would preach their doctrine of naval expansion. They began to send him their memorandums of complaints and plans with the certainty that they could count on him for understanding and cooperation. Roosevelt soon found himself an intermediary between the militant admirals and the peace-seeking Secretary.

To the impetuous Roosevelt, Secretary Daniels seemed undisturbed over war rumblings and imperturbed by inadequate supplies of men and material. Like Wilson, Daniels firmly hoped that peace would prevail, and he was remarkably patient with an assistant secretary who constantly argued for naval expansion and spoke about the likelihood of war.

Although he had little experience on the job, Roosevelt felt from the outset that he was the key man on the team getting things done. When his boss was absent, he served as Acting Secretary and used the opportunity to push through whatever minor measures he could safely sign without incurring Daniels' wrath. The admirals seemed to know when he would be serving as Secretary and saw to it that their pet projects hit his desk at that time.

Though Daniels seemed bumbling and slow-moving to FDR, he was aware of Roosevelt's actions and humored his assistant, letting him think he was responsible for more than he actually was. The Secretary was much more effective than Roosevelt thought. His background as a Southern Democratic leader gave him a position of trust on Capitol Hill and he handled key Congressional leaders and committees with finesse, winning votes for naval bills and emerging in a key liaison position between the President and Congress. That the Navy Secretary enjoyed the complete confidence of the President may explain his remarkable forebearance in the face of Roosevelt's impertinence and criticism.

Along with winning over the admirals, Roosevelt saw that organized labor was the key to running the huge naval establishment with success. He realized that labor needed recognition, and from the outset he built a solid foundation of cordial labor relations. The young politician sensed the importance of the labor vote in oiling a political machine for the future. "You can come to me at any time in my office and we can talk matters over," he told a group of machinists, and hardly a day passed when a labor delegation did not take advantage of his open door. His hard work to win labor trust paid dividends, for at the end of his naval career, Roosevelt could boast that the Navy had not had a single strike during his tenure, an impressive record in view of the fact that more

than two thousand union strikes and lockouts occurred throughout the country in the first seven
months of 1916 alone.

Roosevelt made every effort to attend labor hear-
ings in person or sent his aide, Louis Howe, as a
troubleshooter when strikes threatened. He used his
ingenuity to make shipyards run more smoothly, although various methods of achieving efficiency
aroused violent arguments between labor and management. FDR steered a careful course in those
turbulent waters, refusing to advocate any particular
efficiency system. This kept him on the side of management while winning him the support of labor,
which soon sent out word that Roosevelt was the
man to see to settle wage negotiations, shipyard dis-
putes, and a multitude of petty problems. He was
always willing to listen, check into the matter, and
render assistance if possible.

Roosevelt had a sense of the dramatic and used
this flair on his inspection tours of the shipyards. He
delighted in the production, with marines drawn up
at full attention, Navy bands blaring a fanfare, and
sailors firing a seventeen-gun salute. On each tour he
took great pains to understand local conditions and
commented knowledgeably on them, often winning
favorable headlines and good will along with the
promise of future support from local politicians.

Although they tangled on a score of naval policies,
in one respect both FDR and Daniels were in com-

plete accord. They each had a positive zeal for pinching pennies and agreed on battling monopolistic interests that might profit at the Navy's expense. Daniels was a Southern agrarian and a natural foe of monopolies; Roosevelt was a Northern progressive who fought big business in a determination to stretch every dollar to the utmost to build a bigger Navy. They spent much time in 1913 and 1914 scrutinizing naval contracts to ensure competitive bidding so that the Navy would get full value for what it spent. They took on the formidable task of dealing with steel manufacturers who submitted identical bids and coal mine owners who used lack of competition to raise their prices. By the 1916 campaign FDR could boast that he had saved the Navy more than a million dollars.

But preparedness was always uppermost in his mind. In January, 1914, he said, "Our national defense must extend all over the western hemisphere, must go out a thousand miles into the sea, must embrace the Philippines and over the seas, wherever our commerce may be . . . . We must create a Navy not only to protect our shores and our possessions but our merchant ships in time of war . . . no matter where they may go."

Events proved him right. On a train headed for Pennsylvania where he was scheduled to make a speech on August 1, 1914, he heard the news that Germany had declared war on Russia. "These are history-making days," he wrote hastily to his wife and rushed back to Washington. If he expected the Navy Department to be bustling with war plans, he was mistaken.

He found to his dismay that it was still doing business as usual. President Wilson insisted on a policy of strict neutrality, and Daniels agreed. Impatiently, Roosevelt wrote his wife a few days later that Daniels and Secretary of State William Jennings Bryan had as much conception of what a general European war meant as his four-year-old son Elliott "has of higher mathematics." From then on, he conducted an even more persistent campaign to convince his superiors that war was on the way and that the Navy must be fully prepared.

In 1916 President Wilson asked the nation to be neutral in thought as well as action, but Roosevelt had already made up his mind. "I just know I shall do some awful unneutral thing before I get through!" he told his wife. He tried to convince the President of the need for military preparedness. He pushed universal military training and worked on plans for establishing a Council of National Defense, and throughout the prewar years worked always to educate the public. "Either we want adequate preparedness, or we want none. Half a Navy is worthless," he preached.

By fall of 1916 he was completely blunt. "We've

got to get into the war," he told Daniels. Slowly the people were becoming committed to an Allied victory. The sinking of the *Lusitania* by a German submarine torpedo in May of 1915 had swayed them, and the crisis of further submarine torpedoings now brought public opinion into closer agreement with Roosevelt.

The people were behind President Wilson when he asked Congress in 1916 to pass legislation for substantial increases in the Army, Navy, and Merchant Marine. They still did not want to fight but did accept the necessity for a national defense program. In 1916 Wilson won re-election by a precariously narrow margin on the platform of "He kept us out of war." He still preached negotiated peace and intended to pursue this course.

After the 1916 election some officials actually proposed that Navy Secretary Daniels resign and be replaced by Roosevelt, but Roosevelt wisely repudiated such suggestions even while he continued expressing his frank disgust with government inaction.

World tension increased through the winter, and it became evident that the United States would be pushed into the conflict. By January, 1917, the die was cast, for German military leaders decided to return to unrestricted submarine warfare, although they knew that Wilson had drawn the line at this point. The President vainly hoped for peace and still blocked the Navy from recalling ships from the Caribbean to outfit for war, which Roosevelt urged vehemently.

In March German submarines torpedoed three American ships. Wilson's Cabinet unanimously advised him to ask Congress to declare war, and on the evening of April 2, 1917, Wilson delivered his war message to Congress. "The world must be made safe for democracy," he said. Four days later the nation was at war. Roosevelt's years of advocating preparedness had been vindicated.

He urged Daniels now to speed decision-making, to cut through red tape, and to give careful thought to new ideas that might spur victory. With war finally broken out, Daniels demanded a comprehensive war program and served with distinction while the Navy grew from 54,000 enlisted men in 1916 to 497,000 by the war's end. He also gave Roosevelt more room for ideas and action.

One novel idea Roosevelt promoted was the laying of a mine barrage in the North Sea to keep German submarines out of the Atlantic Ocean. The cost was staggering and technical difficulties almost insurmountable, but through Roosevelt's pressure the mine barrier was laid late in the war. In later years he felt this was a major contribution to Allied victory.

During his naval stint Roosevelt had not completely neglected politics. "I am trying to forget that there is such a thing as politics," he said in 1918, but this was far from the truth.

He had moved into an influential political position when he had gone to the nation's capital, and he intended to use this base to help dispense federal patronage in his home state. The well-paying jobs of local postmasters and customs collectors were prizes to dispense, and Roosevelt began to recommend followers of his progressive wing back home whenever he could. Tammany, however, had long controlled the dispensation of patronage and for the most part maintained control over customs and post office jobs, though Roosevelt did manage through the years to fill some vacant spots in upstate New York.

Rumors had flown in 1914 that he would run for governor. Tammany refused to support him and he could not unite upstate politicians, so he discarded that notion. Instead, he turned hopefully toward the nomination for United States senator.

"Personally, if I were not engaged in this work in the Navy Department, I should like nothing better than to get into the fight actively," he said, throwing out a feeler. Though he got little response, he impulsively announced he would be a candidate in the primaries without checking with his chief political aide and adviser, Louis Howe. Unfortunately, he did not have Tammany's backing, and President Wilson refused to take sides in a battle against the machine.

Tammany chose a distinguished diplomat, James

W. Gerard, a Wilson appointee, as Roosevelt's opposition. Roosevelt lost in the primaries by a two-to-one
ratio, one of the few important political defeats of his
entire career. But in his usual optimistic way, he
bounced back and found some victory in the loss. He
reasoned that he had put his name before the people
and would run better next time. More important to
his future, both FDR and Tammany leaders came to
an important political realization as a result of that
defeat. They learned that they had to set aside their
grievances and call a truce in their political skirmishes
if they were to gain party victories in the future.

Of course, there was no statement of political armistice, but Roosevelt slowly began to let his anti-
Tammany feelings simmer down. Past enmities between the two factions began to fade away, and the
advantages of forming a coalition became clearer. By
1915 Roosevelt found that he could praise the
Tammany-supported Al Smith, and the next year he
supported Tammany's Robert Wagner. Peace was
almost ceremoniously declared on the Fourth of
July, 1917, when Tammany invited its old enemy
Roosevelt to speak at a celebration and sit for a picture with his old foe Boss Charles Murphy.

The machine still had no great affection for the
progressive Roosevelt, but in 1918, when casting
about for a suitable choice for governor, he was
sounded out. Roosevelt probably could have had the
nomination and possibly even the election. But he

turned down the chance. He wisely reasoned that this was a premature offer. He was only thirty-five and in his physical prime. He felt very strongly that he should serve in the armed forces. He itched to get into the battle and saw clearly the political advantages his Cousin Theodore had scored as a result of military service.

Roosevelt asked Daniels to let him resign so he could enter active duty. But Daniels said his country needed him in Washington. Daniels asked the President to persuade his determined assistant secretary to stay. Wilson said sternly, "Tell the young man his only and best war service is to stay where he is."

Of course, FDR had to obey. However, he persuaded his boss to send him overseas to inspect bases. This trip filled his need for adventure, and he relished every minute aboard a destroyer on a shakedown cruise as it zigzagged across the Atlantic through the war zone. The excitement of an alert and sighting a German submarine satisfied his intense yearning to be in the thick of the battle, and later Roosevelt recalled this wartime experience and embellished upon the dangers he had encountered.

Unfortunately, on the way home he fell ill with influenza and had to be taken ashore on a stretcher. By the time he had recovered, the President told him an armistice was in the offing, so the disappointed Roosevelt never fulfilled his deepest wish of wearing the Navy blue.

Throughout those war years, Roosevelt never forgot his role as father of five spirited youngsters. He adored his growing family and arranged moments to romp with them whenever he could. Amid the hectic daily pace of keeping appointments, visiting battleships, witnessing target practice, and entertaining important guests, he would gather up the four little boys and Anna and take them for an outing aboard the *Sylph,* the converted Presidential yacht assigned to the Secretary of the Navy. It was not an unusual sight to see the yacht cruising down the Potomac River to Mount Vernon with happy Roosevelt children tearing around the decks at play.

He called his children "the chicks" and hated to discipline them. He chose rather to be an affectionate partner, playmate, and co-conspirator with them in their fun and games. His lack of sternness may account for the carefree and uninhibited nature of the five; the children had a reputation for dropping water bombs on ladies arriving for tea and shooting off stink bombs during formal dinner parties. Their greatest hero was their father, and they waited always for the wonderful times they spent with him tobogganing at Hyde Park and sailing and swimming at Campobello.

The young politician who was still immature when he had come to Washington had grown up in many ways by the war's end. Long hours, hard bargaining and compromise, tough decisions, endless arguing of his viewpoint, and working together with all types of people and ideas had matured and mellowed him. Physically, too, he had grown older. His body was in superb condition. He could vault over a row of chairs and play fifty-four holes of golf without strain. But wrinkles began to appear on his forehead, his hair began to thin at the temples, and dark shadows began to form circles under his blue eyes.

At the beginning of 1919 he persuaded Daniels to let him go to Europe to complete the Navy's many affairs abroad. While he was at sea, he heard the news that his Cousin Teddy had died. In Paris he and Eleanor sadly attended a memorial service for the former President, and Franklin undoubtedly pondered the fact that he alone now carried the political banner of the Roosevelts.

In Paris they witnessed unforgettable evidence of the popular acclaim of President Wilson for his work in winning the war and planning the Covenant of the proposed League of Nations. They sailed home aboard ship with the triumphant President, but when they got back to America, they watched the tidal wave of cheers dwindle to a tiny ripple and then disappear as Congress repudiated the peace treaty. Wilson retreated broken and ill to the White House.

Through it all, Roosevelt remained a Wilson supporter, although his approach to the League of Nations was somewhat more pragmatic than the President's. "It is important not to dissect the document," he said. "The important thing is first to approve the general plan."

When the League plan failed to pass, Roosevelt turned his attention to other issues. He gave a number of speeches that year on subjects ranging from universal military training and internationalism to the necessity for increased government efficiency in handling the burdens thrust upon it.

Peacetime had come, his job was routine now, and the future was unclear. But 1920, an election year, was just around the corner. His friends were already urging him to run for governor or senator in New York. FDR felt a change in the air. He was ready to move on, to follow in his illustrious cousin's footsteps if he could. He carefully considered what road he should take to attain the destiny that surely could be his.

CHAPTER SIX

★★★★★★

PRELUDE TO THE PRESIDENCY

America moved forward into the new decade of the twenties somewhat reluctantly. People were tired of talk of international responsibility; after the war they had turned their eyes again toward home and yearned for the good old days. Woodrow Wilson's progressivism was no longer attractive, and opposition to the League of Nations grew steadily. A national election was in the offing, the first in which women would be allowed to vote, but most Americans were more concerned with readjusting to peacetime than electing the next President.

They were coping with rising unemployment because wartime controls and contracts had been rapidly scrapped, and because peacetime production had not yet resumed. They were concerned with a rising cost of living, a pile-up of agricultural surpluses, and the argument over the new Prohibition law which forbade the consumption of liquor. A great wave of strikes erupted across the country in

1919, and the tide of public opinion turned against organized labor and groups such as radicals and Communists.

Above all, people wished for peaceful times and a return to normalcy, and this is what the Republicans were counting on to win the election. They felt sure the pendulum would swing their way after the long Democratic reign. They felt no need to nominate their strongest candidate for President, and at the convention they made their choice late one night in a "smoke-filled room." Warren G. Harding of Ohio, a party regular and a thoroughgoing conservative, would run for President on their ticket. His running mate would be Calvin Coolidge. Their campaign platform was ready-made—a "return to normalcy" would swing the voters their way.

The Democrats were in a more difficult position. Their leader, Woodrow Wilson, was an invalid; yet partially paralyzed as he was, he secretly yearned for a third-term nomination. The leaders from the big cities were eager to discard him as their party symbol; they knew that the cause he espoused, the League of Nations Covenant, was a losing issue. Yet Wilson had publicly told his party that this election must be a "solemn referendum" to settle the war.

Into this confusing atmosphere Roosevelt headed on his way to the Democratic convention in San Francisco. He had been elected a full-fledged delegate from his Congressional district and took with him a large entourage to cope with any unexpected situation that might arise.

He had already tackled Tammany to try to abolish the use of the unit rule, which enabled the majority of delegate votes to control the entire state delegation. Despite FDR's convincing arguments, Tammany refused to withdraw the unit rule. At the convention, however, the Rules Committee invalidated the rule, so delegates who had been selected by primary elections could vote independently. Roosevelt finally won his argument.

On the opening day of the convention, as flags were flying and bands were playing in the circus atmosphere of the hall, Roosevelt created such a dramatic sensation with an incident that he immediately gained the notice of all the delegates. The episode occurred when he wanted to show his support for Wilson in a colorful demonstration that was taking place. An enormous portrait of the party leader had been unveiled and a noisy demonstration ensued. Delegates marched through the aisles waving banners and cheering, but the New York delegation, at the insistence of the Tammany chairman, sat still and silent in their seats.

In annoyance Roosevelt tried to persuade the Tammany chairman to march for Wilson. The chairman refused, holding a firm grip on the New York standard. In the hubbub of shouting voices and blowing horns, Roosevelt reached over and grabbed the banner. He wrestled for a moment with the chairman and finally took the banner from him and marched away triumphantly to join the demonstration. The convention crowd watched in amazement and marked young Roosevelt as a man of courage and conviction.

In his most dramatic manner Roosevelt later said, "About half a dozen men grabbed me and we had a jolly fight, but I got the standard and it was paraded."

The convention proceeded for several days in a seesaw battle between three candidates, Governor James M. Cox of Ohio; William G. McAdoo, Wilson's Secretary of the Treasury and son-in-law; and Attorney General A. Mitchell Palmer, a man who had made a name for himself as an anti-Communist prosecutor. The winning candidate had to gain a two-thirds majority of the votes, and the three-way deadlock prevented a quick decision.

Roosevelt seconded the nomination of Governor Al Smith of New York, but when Smith dropped out along with other favorite sons, Roosevelt and other upstate delegates switched their support to McAdoo. McAdoo had been labeled the "crown prince" by those who did not want him as heir apparent to the Wilson program. Cox, pro-Wilson but not identified as a "Wilson man," had been an efficient governor, and was a "Wet" on the important liquor issue and thus acceptable to the liberals. But McAdoo and Palmer ran neck and neck for thirty-eight ballots. It was clear a compromise had to be made. Finally, on the forty-third ballot the city bosses stepped in. They agreed on the anti-Prohibition candidate, Cox, as the compromise most likely to win big-city votes, and he won the nomination on the forty-fourth ballot.

After the Presidential decision, choosing a Vice-Presidential candidate was almost an afterthought. Traditionally, he should balance the ticket. He should come from a different part of the country than the Presidential nominee, and he should represent different interests in the party. In the dawn just after the Presidential nomination, Cox received a call from his manager at the convention. He asked to know who Cox would choose as his running mate. In his autobiography Cox says, "I told him I had given the matter some thought and that my choice would be Franklin D. Roosevelt of New York." Cox did not even know Roosevelt personally, but he felt the New Yorker met the geographical requirement, was known as an independent, and had a famous name. He might even bring some progressive votes over from the Republican camp who had always voted for Teddy.

Cox was a political pro. He had his manager contact Boss Murphy to confirm his choice. Murphy was delighted to be consulted. "I don't like Roosevelt," he said. "He is not well-known in the country . . . but . . . this is the first time a Democratic nominee for the Presidency has shown me courtesy. That's why I would vote for the devil himself if Cox wanted me to. Tell him we will nominate Roosevelt on the first ballot as soon as we assemble."

And so the choice was made. Word spread over the convention floor that Cox and Murphy wanted Roosevelt. Al Smith rose to his feet and seconded FDR's nomination for the Vice-Presidency. Other names were quickly withdrawn. And without further discussion Franklin Roosevelt was placed on the ticket by acclamation.

When he arrived home at Hyde Park, he told the happy crowd that greeted him how astonished he had been to receive the nomination. "I was sent from the floor of the convention to meet a man under the speaker's platform. The man whom I was supposed to meet was not there. Someone rushed up to me and said, 'They are nominating you.' I replied, 'Quit your kidding.' No one was more surprised than I was to get the Vice-Presidential nomination."

Though he may have been somewhat surprised, Roosevelt quickly assessed the possibilities and saw an opportunity to build a national reputation and win over the multitudes for some future election. When this campaign was past, he planned that the name Roosevelt would come forth naturally whenever Democrats would undertake a search for fresh men for future leadership. Franklin had the example of his cousin Theodore before him, and like Teddy's Vice-Presidency, this was his golden opportunity.

The Presidential and Vice-Presidential nominees conferred immediately on a party platform. Rumblings and outright warnings issued from the Democratic high command that a battle over approving a League Covenant would be a mistake and should be avoided. The people were weary of the issue, they felt, and their feelings proved to be right. However, both Cox and Roosevelt sincerely believed that the League should be the focal point of the campaign.

Shortly after their strategy talk, they made a pilgrimage to the White House to visit the ailing President. Wilson sat in a wheelchair, his paralyzed left arm covered with a shawl, and the men must have realized that the nation's leader was seriously ill. In a weak voice the President thanked Cox and FDR for paying him a call. Then Cox said, "Mr. Wilson, I have always admired you for your fight for the League of Nations . . . we are going to be a million per cent with you, and your Administration, and that means the League of Nations."

It was an emotion-packed session. The President was deeply touched and summoned up enough strength to say, "I am very grateful. I am very grateful."

So the Democratic campaign strategy was settled despite the advice of the leaders and FDR's own aides. The central theme would be support of the League and progressivism, even though this did not promise popular backing. Meanwhile, the Republicans concentrated on appealing to the people. They made few speeches and fewer promises. They advocated a "return to normalcy." Harding had only to sit on his porch and await the expected landslide in his favor.

Roosevelt formulated his own course of action. He must be identified with a vision of the future, he reasoned, and with internationalism and progressivism, though his advisers insisted the voters were weary of these issues. His way was to run an aggressive campaign, full of vigor and energy and good spirits, and entirely separate from that of Presidential-nominee Cox.

He stood on the front steps of his Hyde Park home and in a ringing voice emphasized youth and progress in his acceptance speech. "We can never go back," he said. "The 'good old days' are gone forever; we have no regrets. For our eyes are trained ahead— forward to better new days. . . . To this future I dedicate myself." The clear voice, few gestures, and resounding words captured the confidence of his first audience as they would throughout the campaign.

He took to the road immediately in a backbreaking schedule of speeches and stops in backwaters and big towns, whistle-stops, and quiet villages. He usually traveled in a railroad car attached to a regularly scheduled train, sometimes by automobile, once by airplane, moving across the country to spread the word of the Democratic party. He spoke from dawn till midnight, averaging seven speeches a day in a

wide arc through the northwest in August, swinging
through New England and New York in September,
returning west to Colorado, and finally concentrating
on influential New York State toward the end of the
campaign trail. He wound up at Madison Square
Garden at the end of October for a huge rally after
more than a thousand speaking engagements.

In the process, the Roosevelt image was stamped
indelibly on crowd after crowd who heard his persuasive voice. Just as important, he gathered together an experienced and dedicated staff who would
work for him for many years. Missy LeHand, Miss
Grace Tully, Stephen Early, and Marvin McIntyre,
all his faithful workers for many years, were re-
cruited on this campaign.

"We must go forward or flounder," he preached.
Most frequently he spoke up for the League, though
his audience responded with indifference to the subject. He talked on other subjects, too, concentrating
on tariff issues, lashing out at excessive campaign
spending by the Republicans, and criticizing the
control of Harding by a small gang of men. Certain
themes began to appear that formed the nucleus of
programs he would espouse as President in the thirties: better marketing facilities and living conditions
for impoverished farmers, greater conservation of
natural resources, and improved relations with our
neighbors to the south.

The Republican opposition began to sense that the

Democratic Roosevelt was capturing the popularity once owned by their great hero, the Republican Roosevelt. They tried to stem the flow of enthusiasm he generated before it was too late to stop him from stepping into the Rough Rider's boots and riding off with Teddy Roosevelt's fame. They sent out a scout, Teddy's son, who they figured would be able to slow down the tide because he had the magic name himself. Theodore, Jr., traveled westward and said, "He is a maverick. He does not have the brand of our family." But Teddy's son was too late. In October Franklin said confidently, "I wish Theodore Roosevelt were alive today. He at least had definite convictions." He could praise Teddy as a fair fighter, as an example to American youth, knowing full well that people were making a comparison of the two.

FDR's personality came across easily to the people. One friendly reporter described his public reception: "He gets . . . the last ounce of appeal-power out of each sentence. . . . The physical impression leaves nothing to be asked—the figure of an idealized college football player, almost the poster type in public life."

Unfortunately, there were times when FDR did not show himself to such good advantage. In August, in a speech in Butte, Montana, he committed a political blunder that hung over his head for years. In the middle of a speech on Central America, he boasted, "You know I have had something to do with the running of a couple of little republics. The facts are that I wrote Haiti's constitution myself and, if I do say it, I think it a pretty good constitution."

He was referring to an official trip he had made while on Navy business when the U.S. marines had occupied Haiti. The casual remark was unfortunate, for the Republicans seized upon it and pointed to it with alarm as an outright insult to Latin America. They referred to it and pointed out the U.S. occupation as "one of the blackest records of dishonor in the history of military imperialism" under Wilson's Administration. Roosevelt at first denied the statement. Then when he saw the fuss it was causing, he resorted to the classic ruse of saying he had been misquoted, and that Republican reporters and editors had twisted his words.

As a result of this 1920 campaign one thing became clear. Though he was to lose in this election, he was beginning to find a strategy for future victory. He had a glimpse of the importance of uniting the West and South and tying them to progressivism, and he concentrated particularly upon the West in his speechmaking, for it was Westerners especially who regarded Teddy Roosevelt as one of the greatest Presidents and they were enthusiastic about his cousin FDR.

As election day approached, the Vice-Presidential hopeful headed home to await the voting results. The outcome unfortunately was just as predicted—

disastrous for the Democrats. The Republicans won a sweeping victory, as Harding polled more than twice as many votes as Cox in Roosevelt's New York State alone. All in all, they won by over seven million votes. The GOP triumphed, 16,152,220 to 9,147,553, and won both Senate and House control. The people had repudiated Wilsonian progressivism and now anticipated a "return to normalcy."

FDR lost the Vice-Presidency but in defeat he won a larger victory. He had traveled the country, establishing contacts and friendships wherever he had gone, had advised Democrats to start reorganizing for the next campaign, and had captured for himself a dominant voice in the party's future.

Three days after the election he wrote, "Curiously enough, I do not feel in the least bit down-hearted . . . As long as the other people were going to win I am glad they have such a clear majority. The whole responsibility will be theirs, and I hope they will be able to make good for the sake of the country."

To his aide, Steve Early, he wrote that he was not through but just beginning. "Thank the Lord we are both comparatively youthful," he wrote with an eye intent on winning future elections.

CHAPTER SEVEN

★ ★ ★ ★ ★ ★

A CRIPPLING DISASTER

The morning was clear, fresh, and sunny at Campobello Island that August day of 1921. Roosevelt and his friend Van Lear Black jumped aboard Black's yacht, the *Sabalo*, for a carefree day of fishing after sailing up the coast together on a return trip from Washington.

FDR was bone-weary, he suddenly realized. He had just completed the difficult ordeal of preparing testimony for an unfriendly Republican Senate committee that was trying to stir up scandal in Wilson's old Navy Department. In the hot, sticky Washington July weather FDR had worked around the clock to counteract an unfavorable statement prematurely released to the press by the Republicans before listening to Roosevelt testify on supposed Navy wrongdoings. But now in the brisk refreshing air of northern Maine as Roosevelt gazed out toward the dramatic rocky shoreline and the white-capped waves, the whole unpleasant incident receded in his mind and he relaxed once again.

The future looked bright indeed. He had become a vice-president of the Fidelity and Deposit Company of Maryland, one of the country's largest surety bonding firms, where he was placed in charge of New York operations. His friend Black, who was president of Fidelity, had recognized in his ship-board companion a man with zest and flair, a sports-man like himself, and a potential capitalist who could operate the New York office with executive skill such as he had applied to his job in the Navy Department. FDR's many political contacts would no doubt also help win accounts for the firm and would certainly make him well worth the $25,000 salary the company paid him.

Even with this exciting position, Roosevelt had not at all moved out of the political circle in which he had always traveled. He had ample time now to cul-tivate new contacts and renew old ones. He intended to use a new law partnership with his friends Gren-ville T. Emmet and Langdon P. Marvin as a base of operations, both political and economic. He had every intention of participating in the prosperous financial life of the twenties. From his office on Wall Street he proposed to take full advantage of the rich years of golden prosperity he foresaw in the next decade.

But right now fishing took up his attention. He

was on a well-earned vacation, and it was clear he needed this rest, this chance to renew his vitality and buoyancy, to romp on the island with the children, play golf, and fish in the sparkling water.

As the yacht headed out into the bay, he started across deck to bait his fishhook. Suddenly he lost his balance and before he knew what had happened, he slipped across the deck and fell overboard. Though he quickly broke the fall and hardly submerged, he splashed into the icy water. He came up gasping for breath, instantly chilled to the bone. The water was so cold it almost seemed paralyzing. He hastily climbed aboard again. Drying off in the summer sun, FDR dismissed the incident and continued to enjoy a day of relaxation and fishing.

The next day, Wednesday, August 10, another typically beautiful day at Campobello, Roosevelt came down to breakfast eager to join the children for a day of sailing and games. His idea of leisure had always been to bound from one activity to another, and this day was no exception. Everyone set out for a sail in their small sailboat but almost as soon as they had gotten onto the water they spotted a spiral of smoke rising from a nearby island.

"Forest fire," the boys shouted, and FDR headed toward the island to combat it. They beached the boat and ran to the site of the fire, setting to work at beating the flames with evergreen branches. Several hours later when the blaze was finally extinguished, they rested, grimy, exhausted, with eyes smarting and muscles aching from their effort.

By the time they got back to Campobello, Roosevelt still did not feel quite recuperated. "Let's go for a quick dip at the lagoon," he suggested. He figured their favorite swimming spot would as always cure him of his vague feeling of tiredness.

He led the way with his sons trotting behind for the two miles across the island until they reached the freezing water of the lagoon and jumped in. After all this exertion, they arrived home, and a pile of newspapers and mail caught FDR's attention. He sat reading his mail, still in his wet bathing suit.

Of that plunge into the chilly water, he later said, "I didn't feel the same reaction, the glow I'd expected. When I reached the house the mail was in, with several newspapers I hadn't seen. I sat reading for awhile, too tired even to dress. I'd never felt quite that way before."

During supper, he felt more chilled and finally went to bed. The next morning he awoke with aching pains in his legs and back and a fever.

"When I swung out of bed my left leg lagged but I managed to move about and to shave," he recounted later. "I tried to persuade myself that the trouble with my leg was muscular, that it would disappear as I used it. But presently one leg refused to work, and then the other."

When daughter Anna came into his bedroom,

FDR smiled and made a cheerful joke. She could not guess the pain he was already enduring.

The family had planned to head off on a wilderness camping trip with their father that day. Eleanor saw how ill her husband was and thought it might be a good thing to send the children off as planned. Completely worried by now, she sent over to the mainland for the doctor in Lubec. Dr. Bennett came and examined Roosevelt, diagnosing his illness as a common cold despite the severe pain and unusual paralysis that was setting in.

The next morning, August 12, Roosevelt was in complete agony. He could not stand and by nightfall had lost all power to move his legs. They were numb yet extremely sensitive to the touch, and every inch of his body ached. He began to realize with growing apprehension that he was partly paralyzed from the chest down. Eleanor was growing frantic. She ministered to him all day and all night, but by Saturday she and Louis Howe agreed they must find another doctor.

They checked the resorts all around and finally found Dr. W. W. Keen from Philadelphia, vacationing nearby. Dr. Keen thought the paralysis was caused by a blood clot in the lower spinal cord and recommended heavy massage. The two set to work alternately massaging FDR's legs, heavily kneading the limbs and feet, though the pain was excruciating with each touch. Little could they imagine that this massage was the worst possible treatment for FDR's damaged muscles.

Despite all their efforts, his temperature continued to soar, and for a time he fell into despair at his helplessness and pain. After a week of illness, his temperature began to drop and in spite of his inability to control his legs, his spirits began to revive somewhat.

A full two weeks after the onset of the perplexing disability, and after two mistaken diagnoses, a Boston specialist on polio, Dr. Robert W. Lovett, arrived at the island. He examined Roosevelt and recognized the symptoms he knew so well. It was poliomyelitis, he said, a mild attack, and Roosevelt might recover completely. He ordered Eleanor to stop the massages immediately and recommended hot baths.

During the ordeal, Roosevelt had been first in the depths of depression, feeling that God had abandoned him, but with Eleanor's courage, cheerfulness, and tender ministrations combined with his own natural optimism, his faith returned. When Dr. Lovett told him recovery was possible, this was the turning point. He grasped the hope with tenacity and determination and resolved to maintain a cheerful attitude no matter what.

Meanwhile, Eleanor had the unpleasant duty of informing the family of the catastrophe that had struck. Louis Howe had carefully withheld all news of the illness from the press until a proper diagnosis

Above, an early photograph of Franklin Delano Roosevelt, taken in February, 1883, and below, Franklin Roosevelt, in 1889, on "Debby," his first pony. (FRANKLIN D. ROOSEVELT LIBRARY)

Roosevelt, center, with members of the second football team at Groton, 1899. Below, Roosevelt with the senior board of the Harvard Crimson, 1904. (FRANKLIN D. ROOSEVELT LIBRARY)

A portrait of Franklin with his mother and father, taken in May, 1899. (FRANKLIN D. ROOSEVELT LIBRARY)

Eleanor and Franklin Roosevelt after their marriage on March 17, 1905. (FRANKLIN D. ROOSEVELT LIBRARY) *The photograph below of the Roosevelt family was taken while the family visited Campobello Island in 1920. Franklin and Eleanor flank Mrs. Sara Roosevelt; the children are, left to right, Elliott, Franklin, Jr., John, Anna, and James.* (UNITED PRESS INTERNATIONAL)

Roosevelt takes the oath of office for the second term as governor of New York, December, 1930. (FRANKLIN D. ROOSEVELT LIBRARY) *Below, President Roosevelt addressing the nation during a fireside chat.* (UNITED PRESS INTERNATIONAL)

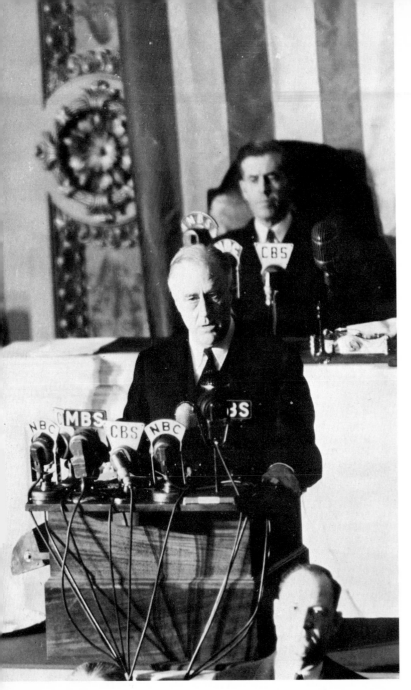

FDR before Congress, asking for the declaration of war. (UNITED
PRESS INTERNATIONAL)

With Churchill in 1945. (U.S. SIGNAL CORPS)

Above, FDR and Churchill with members of the Pacific War Council in Washington, June, 1942. Below, FDR meets with Churchill and Stalin at Yalta, February 9, 1945. (FRANKLIN D. ROOSEVELT LIBRARY)

could be made and until they had decided what should be done. Howe managed to keep the news a secret until August 27, seventeen days after the initial attack. Then he announced that FDR was improving and that there would be no permanent effect from the polio.

Now Eleanor wrote to Roosevelt's mother, who had been vacationing in Europe. "Dearest Mama, Franklin has been quite ill and so can't go down to meet you on Tuesday to his great regret, but Uncle Fred and Aunt Kassie both write they will be there so it will not be a lonely homecoming. We are so happy to have you home again dear, you don't know what it means to feel you are near again."

In mid-September, a month after the illness had struck, Dr. Lovett finally gave permission for him to be moved from the island to New York's Presbyterian Hospital where his convalescence might begin. Roosevelt was still flat on his back, unable to turn over or move his legs. Louis Howe had the grim task of transporting a man in pain on a stretcher from the island to a private railroad car on the mainland. He wanted to accomplish this in secret, so the press could not see that FDR was really seriously ill.

Howe carefully planned every step of the move as though he were a general on the battlefield. Roosevelt was slipped onto a stretcher in his bedroom, carried down a rocky slope to the beach, and lifted onto a waiting launch. The children, only vaguely aware of the illness that had struck their once vigorous father, stood openmouthed as they watched him carried helplessly out of the house. When he saw their uncertainty and fright, Roosevelt waved to them cheerfully and smiled to reassure his "chicks."

Each jostle of the stretcher gave him a knifelike stab of pain as he was lifted off the launch at the mainland dock, bundled onto a baggage cart, and jogged along to the waiting train. There he gritted his teeth for the grimmest task of all as he was painfully hoisted through the open train window. Then he was quickly settled comfortably before the crowd could spot him.

Incredible as it seems, this entire maneuver was completed in secrecy. Howe had intentionally leaked the rumor to the press that FDR would be landed at a dock at the far end of town, while he intended to dock him at the near end. By the time the reporters caught up with their quarry, he was calmly settled in the railway car, almost jauntily smoking a cigarette. One newspaper correspondent said, "Mr. Roosevelt was enjoying his cigarette and had a good appetite. Although unable to sit up, he says he is feeling more comfortable." So Howe's ruse worked as planned, and curious readers were given no inkling as to the real seriousness of FDR's polio attack at the time.

Once settled in the hospital and under the care of Dr. George Draper, an old Groton schoolmate, and Dr. Lovett, Roosevelt began his long convalescence.

The public now found out what had happened. He had contracted poliomyelitis, Howe stated matter-of-factly. The attack had paralyzed the legs below the knees. But Howe predicted a recovery, and *The New York Times* quoted the doctor as saying that hs patient would not be crippled, for no one need fear permanent injury from the attack.

This strategy of minimizing the severity of the attack and stressing a complete recovery actually worked too well. People assumed that FDR would be in the thick of the political battle immediately, and when one invitation to attend a meeting soon arrived, Howe wrote a bit sarcastically, "Mr. Pell had better wake up and hear the birdies!"

Dr. Lovett's first opinion was that "it was a mild case within the range of possible complete recovery and evidently not of the severest type." But sadly, he had to write to his associate a letter saying, "I am much concerned at the very slow recovery both as regards the disappearance of pain, which is very generally present, and as to the recovery of even slight power to twitch the muscles . . . the lower extremities present a most distressing picture."

The doctor realized the importance of the psychological frame of mind of his patient to even partial recovery. "He has such courage, such ambition, and yet at the same time such an extraordinarily sensitive emotional mechanism that it will take all the skill which we can muster to lead him successfully to a recognition of what he really faces without crushing him," the doctor concluded.

Yet in all his pain, FDR held onto his extraordinary optimism and gallant refusal to face defeat. He fully believed it was a mild attack of paralysis, and he relied on the doctor to release him from the hospital in a few weeks, at least on crutches. He rigged up an overhead strap so that he could pull himself up and turn over, and he started calling in his secretary to work on writing letters, cataloging his collection of naval history, and putting his stamp collection in order. Despite his optimism, the stark diagnosis "not improving" had to be written on his medical charts by the end of October when he was finally released to go home.

He returned to his house on 65th Street as an invalid, able only to pull himself up on a strap and maneuver himself into a wheelchair. That in itself was great progress, but his goal had been much greater—to be up on crutches and walking without a limp by spring. He absolutely insisted that with massive determination and undaunted willpower, the illness could be conquered. And so he set out to win his battle over polio.

It was a bleak winter of family struggle. Eleanor and Howe had joined forces against FDR's mother. Sara Roosevelt was determined that her son Franklin should retire from political activity to the serenity of Hyde Park, and there remain with her for the rest of his life, a gentleman and retired invalid. Although Eleanor had never liked Louis Howe, she joined with him at this most crucial point in FDR's life. They knew full well that if Sara weakened her son's incentive to fight and persuaded him to retire to the life of a country gentleman, it would be a tragic waste of talent. Fortunately, Roosevelt himself refused to give in to his mother's fussing. Refusing pity, never complaining and always cheerful, he set to work at home with a busy routine directed at keeping up his political activities while working to get well.

From the beginning of this unexpected ordeal, FDR had every intention of resuming his full life. Two weeks after polio struck, while he was lying helpless, wracked with pain, and vainly trying to wiggle even his big toe, he authorized the president of Vassar College to name him to a committee to work on an endowment drive. Shortly after that he accepted a spot on the Executive Committee of the Democratic party of New York State.

Now that he was finally home, he determined to organize his life to be able to carry on his political correspondence while concentrating every ounce of strength on walking again.

The house was crowded that winter, and tension and irritation broke the surface quiet as he endeavored to get well. The five lively Roosevelt children did not completely comprehend the extent of their father's illness and sometimes got too rough playing with him. They felt the tenseness of the household as life centered on an invalid father who conducted politics and business at home with a steady stream of secretaries, visitors, and businessmen flowing through the house.

Eleanor undoubtedly bore the brunt of this struggle to rescue her husband for a normal life. With a nurse and Howe living in, she was left without a moment of privacy or even a bedroom of her own. She was always on the move, soothing over difficulties, calming upset children, planning the days so that they would have a semblance of normalcy in their hectic home.

But the new year brought more pain to Roosevelt. The muscles behind his knees began to tighten, and his legs bent double beneath him. The doctor was forced to put his legs in plaster casts, and every day he endured excruciating agony as the cast was chipped away at the back and a wedge driven in, deeper each day. This process gradually stretched his leg muscles until they were straight once again.

By February he could be fitted for braces, heavy and cumbersome affairs made of steel and weighing seven pounds each. These he learned to lock into position to make his legs rigid, and then he learned how to balance so that he could stand with the aid of crutches. Incredibly strong in his belief that he would get well, he practiced on the braces and crutches day by day, doing exercises to rebuild the useless leg muscles.

By the end of that long winter, the strain of Eleanor's constant efforts to keep peace was too much for her. One day, as she sat reading to her sons, she suddenly began to sob and could not stop. Frantically, she hunted out an empty room, locked herself in, and cried until she felt she could cry no more. Gradually, she grew calm again. She bathed her swollen face, returned to the children, and never again, even in the most troubled times of her husband's Presidency, did she fall into such an emotional mood that uncontrollable tears came.

By spring Roosevelt convinced his mother that he had no intention of retiring to the country though he wished to return to Hyde Park frequently. Eleanor and Howe emerged victorious in their fight to win a useful life for FDR. His readjustment to his new way of life was complete. He was now continuing many of his former involvements in politics and business, dropping those that required impossible commitments.

Before polio struck, he had been involved in many activities, ranging from being an Overseer of Harvard University to serving as Chairman of the Greater New York Committee of the Boy Scouts. He kept his name before the public by retaining some of these connections, and in other cases wrote letters or composed speeches for others to read for him.

He knew he would not be able to get about for

awhile, and as a subsitute for his own presence at meetings, he and Howe came up with an inspired alternate—his wife. She began to make political appearances for her husband, representing him especially at women's groups. Soon she began to speak before audiences, an activity that the shy Eleanor had formerly shunned. Before a few years passed, she had become such a knowledgeable campaigner that she was totally involved in FDR's political work.

As a result of all this activity, FDR's recuperation was considered to be inevitable by everyone and he was considered a potential candidate for political office. That spring the party considered him for the U.S. Senate, and one important newspaper suggested him for governor. This had a tremendous effect upon FDR. He knew he was still badly crippled, but with such public support, he could concentrate on getting well with the realization that his political career was not at an end.

The summer of 1922 at Hyde Park was one of patient exercise on trapezes and pulleys and swimming in the sunshine to work his leg muscles. He rigged up an exercise board and parallel bars with a round base, and everyone marveled as they watched him literally drag himself back and forth by sheer physical strength on the bars. His goal by summer's end was to reach the distant gateposts at the end of the long driveway, a quarter-of-a-mile away.

Day by day Roosevelt inched his way along the

drive, balancing precariously on crutches and braces, determined to make the entire walk on his own. He would joke and chat cheerfully with companions, though they could observe at a glance, from the smiling face covered with perspiration and shirt wringing wet, the immense effort he was making. When he could not drag himself another step, he would drop exhausted into a wheelchair and be pushed back. Roosevelt did not make it to the end of the driveway that summer, but he did not give up his effort.

After such exertion, he swam with relief. Water was soothing, he found, and he would swim in the pond in the woods or in a neighbor's pool, and he felt a lightness in his body and freedom he did not feel on land. "Water got me into this fix, and water has to get me out again!" he would say. Later he would turn to water as the most hopeful cure for poliomyelitis.

He spent hours at quiet activities, making model boats, working on his hobbies, or sitting unselfconsciously with his children showing them his pencil-thin legs and identifying the various muscles.

By the end of summer he was tanned from swimming, and his arms and shoulders were on the way to the massive development they acquired through extended strenuous use.

As autumn came, he looked forward to getting back to the city. It was time to cross another threshold, to get back to his office on Wall Street if only for a few hours a day.

Amazingly, this entire ordeal of illness had interrupted the momentum of his expanding political influence for only a few weeks. But it had vast implications on his whole political future and to the development of his character. Perhaps its most important result was the postponement of his immediate political ambitions. His goal had long been determined— he would someday run for the Presidency of the United States—and the onslaught of polio brought no change in this ambition. But in order to win this grand prize, he must hold some prior office, senator or governor, from the most populous state in the union. Only in such a way could he prove that the disaster that had crippled his legs had not killed his political force or cramped his style.

The years of golden prosperity in the early 1920's were not the best times to run as a Democrat. FDR's illness delayed his return to politics until a more appropriate moment. When the pendulum had swung back, when the popularity of the Republicans had run full course, and when the Democrats' moment had returned, he would hopefully be recovered and ready to run for office again.

Meanwhile, his illness added depth and dimension to his character. His self-control, his optimism, his confidence in himself, and his sympathy for others were strengthened and matured. He had suffered through a terrible ordeal and would never again be free from its effects. But he battled with all his strength of mind and body, and he knew he could win.

CHAPTER EIGHT

★ ★ ★ ★ ★ ★

A DIFFICULT COMEBACK

The Fidelity and Deposit Company office at 120 Broadway had one single step leading into the building. Any person with normal use of his legs could walk up the step without a thought. But for FDR one step was a great obstacle that took complete concentration.

His car would pull up before the building, and he would ease out the door, make his way over the step on crutches, and painfully move along the polished marble-floored lobby toward his office. One day that fall of 1922, his rubber-tipped crutch slipped and he crashed heavily to the floor. Gazing up at the bystanders who stared with concern, he spotted one healthy-looking young man, smiled, and beckoned offhandedly for help in getting up. Incidents like this did not stop a man grimly determined to resume a normal life.

He usually came to work for a few hours a day to concentrate on building up the company. He was good at using friends and contacts in winning new business, and by 1924 he reported that Fidelity had made substantial gains of over three million dollars, far more than its competitor.

Since it was difficult for him to make his way to the office of his other business, the law partnership, and since he was not interested in the type of law his partners practiced, he ended that relationship in 1924. In the meantime he had become acquainted with a dynamic young lawyer, Basil O'Connor, whose office was conveniently located in the Fidelity building. O'Connor, eager to become Roosevelt's partner, promised him a guaranteed income of $10,000 a year. This was an attractive offer, for Roosevelt's family commitments and expensive illness had taken its toll on his financial resources. This law partnership worked well from the start, even though Roosevelt did little actual work for the firm.

Like most of his associates in the twenties, Roosevelt had a consuming interest in making money. He regularly bought and sold securities, sometimes gambling on schemes that proved unsuccessful. He could not be called a financial genius although at times he did earn a profit. He sought out unique approaches, novel ideas, or new gadgets that might succeed. He became involved in imaginative schemes ranging from dirigible companies and automated vending machines to a lobster operation which cost him

$26,000 before he could get out. When a clubwoman asked FDR to donate a white elephant to some charitable benefit, Louis Howe, with his usual barbed wit, advised, "Why not send them your stock in the lobster company—that comes under this head!"

These risky ventures showed his enthusiasm and faith in the future, as he plunged wholeheartedly into the heady business atmosphere of the twenties. But business did not satisfy his abundant energy. He looked to other places to provide an outlet for his idealism—and to keep his name before the people.

He became President of the American Construction Council, a trade association set up to encourage voluntary self-regulation and a code of ethics in the building industry. Though he headed the organization for six years, he was often frustrated in attempts to build a better public image for the industry.

His concern for business ethics led him also to serve as chairman of a Committee on Legal Education and Standards of Professional Conduct of the National Crime Commission, another job he could handle without attending many meetings. He worked to raise money for the Woodrow Wilson Foundation established to honor the former President by recognizing distinguished public service. These were worthwhile pursuits that kept him in the public eye and prepared him for the time when he would again run for office.

Meanwhile, the political picture had altered in

August, 1923, when Republican President Harding died suddenly and Calvin Coolidge took office. Coolidge, a man of integrity and conservatism, became President just in time to avoid the repercussions of a major scandal brewing in the Harding Administration when the Teapot Dome oil affair was exposed. In an atmosphere of prosperity and a Republican reminder to "Keep Cool with Coolidge," the 1924 Democratic convention approached.

The Democrats had made a comeback in the 1922 elections. But the party was bitterly split between the rural and urban, Wet and Dry factions, and the 1924 convention only intensified their disunity.

FDR hoped to heal the wounds of the party at the 1924 convention. After a long cruise aboard a houseboat in Florida waters that winter, he felt healthier, stronger, and ready to work. He had supported Al Smith's successful bid for governor in 1922, and for the next few years of the middle 1920's his political ambitions would be inextricably tied up with the "gorgeous knight of the brown derby and the cocked cigar"—the four-term governor of New York. In the spring he had accepted the job as manager for Smith's preconvention campaign to win the Presidential nomination.

Smith, the son of Irish immigrants, had risen out of the slums of the lower East Side and a job in the Fulton Fish Market to become a Tammany-supported political power. Natty in dress, with a lively wit and breezy personality, he stood for social welfare liberalism, sought a progressive Democratic party, fought Prohibition, and perhaps most important, was a Catholic. He and FDR were unlikely partners in politics but were aware that their political fortunes entwined and they had forged a workable political alliance.

Working for Smith's nomination that spring, Roosevelt learned much about the process of securing the party bid for national office. He witnessed firsthand the confused crosscurrents and factions that decided the party's choice. He set up a massive letter-writing campaign and collected information on personalities and politics of the delegates and in the process gathered a storehouse of information invaluable for future campaigns.

The Democratic convention in New York City in June of 1924 brought the antagonistic urban and rural factions of the party face to face in open warfare, and before a compromise candidate emerged from the fray, the party was torn apart and reduced to the laughingstock of the nation. Only one hero emerged unscathed—Franklin D. Roosevelt.

The convention floor at Madison Square Garden was crowded with delegates milling about in noise and confusion. It was almost impossible to push through the throngs, but somehow delegate FDR managed, with son Jimmy's strong arm, to get through the jam of people to his place. He sat, intent

on his speech that would nominate Smith, hoping
that he could persuade the party to unite for victory.
Smith's opponent, William McAdoo, had lost support
when he was hired as legal counsel to Edward
Doheny, a participant in the Teapot Dome affair,
and Smith backers hoped for an early nomination.
They were destined for disappointment, for the emo-
tion-fraught issues of liquor, the Catholic Church,
and the Ku Klux Klan brought such bitterness and
fighting that peace was impossible.

When the moment for Roosevelt's speech arrived,
he headed slowly for the platform, head erect and
smiling, holding his son's arm for support. This was
his first important speech since polio had struck, and
his future hinged on its success. As he approached
the platform, he suddenly realized he would have to
place his entire weight against the rostrum. He wondered if it would support him.

"Shake the rostrum," he commanded a nearby
delegate before he dared lean against it. As the audience gave him a tremendous ovation, he smiled, and
then he began his speech of nomination.

"You equally who come from the great cities of the
East and from the plains and hills of the West, from
the slopes of the Pacific and from the homes and
fields of the Southland, I ask you in all sincerity, in
balloting on that platform tomorrow, to keep first in
your hearts and minds the words of Abraham Lin-

coln: 'With malice toward none, with charity to all.' " In his speech he coined the phrase which would be used to describe Smith from then on—the "Happy Warrior of the political battlefield."

Will Rogers described what happened at the end of the speech. When FDR "did get to the end and named Al, you would have thought somebody had thrown a wildcat in your face. The galleries went wild and about ten state delegations marched and hollered for an hour," Rogers reported.

However, the spectacle that followed the dignified speech reflected little credit on the Democrats. In ballot after ballot Smith and McAdoo remained deadlocked. After days of bitter argument and fighting on the floor and in the gallery, finally on the one hundred and third ballot the warring factions gave up and chose a compromise candidate, John W. Davis, a corporation lawyer.

If there was any winner at all, it was Roosevelt. Walter Lippmann said, "There never was a better political battle nor one in which the spirit of a gentleman and a good sport rose so clearly above faction and hatred." The New York *World* praised him: "He was a gallant and generous figure at all times, and by sheer force of his personality did more to offset the unsportsmanlike and often brutal behavior of some of those in the galleries than any other man."

Throughout the country he had won public admiration for his loyalty to Smith, for his eloquence, and for his call for moderation in the face of fierce party disunity.

The general elections went as predicted. Coolidge won 54 per cent of the vote, Robert La Follette running as a Progressive party candidate took 16.5 per cent, and Davis won only 28.8 per cent. The only consolation to the party was that Smith ran later that year for governor of New York and won—defeating Roosevelt's kin, Theodore Roosevelt, Jr., who also had been Assistant Secretary of the Navy. The defeat marked the end of the Republican Roosevelt's political aspirations.

To the public FDR had shown great spirit and a seemingly healthy body. His participation in active politics had lifted his morale, and he had enjoyed the convention maneuvers tremendously. "It did me no harm and has actually put more pep into my legs than I ever had before," he said. But when people talked about his availability for office, he realized only too well that he could not run until his legs had regained their strength. He knew he must turn his attention in two directions: he must rebuild the wasted leg muscles and at the same time rebuild the torn fragments of his political party.

There must be a rejuvenation, he concluded, a reform of party organization and a rethinking of its goals. He wanted an appeal to idealistic progressivism to be the focal point of reform, and late that year sent out three thousand letters to party leaders asking their opinion on improving the party. Sensing that the national committee would not go along with his belief that the party needed overhaul, he sent the letters directly to local leaders and convention delegates.

He was deluged with differing opinions. Southerners complained about liberalism, Westerners about excessive urban control, Easterners about anti-Catholics and anti-Prohibitionists. Despite the conflict of ideas and divergence of opinion, Roosevelt concluded there was a real desire for more leadership in a liberal direction. He began to advocate a program that would aid farmers, appeal to the growing middle class, and consider the plight of the poor. To mull over the issues, he proposed a national Democratic conference, but suspicious party leaders saw this as a bid on his part for national leadership. They stymied his efforts.

Despite the indirect rebuff and without an elected base, his influence grew as he continued to build a following and make political friends by extensive correspondence with leaders all over the country.

In the meantime, he had not given up hope that he would somewhere find a cure for his wasted legs. He listened eagerly when someone suggested a particular elixir, and tried electric belts, tricycle contraptions, and even horseback riding. He finally concluded that ordinary sunshine and warm water offered the most hope. He had enjoyed the 1923 winter cruise along the Florida coast so much that he and a friend joined in buying a houseboat. For three winters from 1924 to 1926, he sailed aboard the *Larooco* with family and friends, enjoying restful and fun-filled days. But he found the expense not worth the effort, and the *Larooco*'s fate was decided when a 1926 hurricane tore her loose from her moorings and deposited her in ruins several miles away.

The summer of 1925, he thought he had found a cure. He went to Massachusetts and stayed with a doctor who had developed a walking board for polio patients. Without braces Roosevelt practiced endlessly on the board and felt he was making progress. One evening at a dinner party he demonstrated dramatically one useful thing he had learned during his stay there. He and Eleanor were dining with friends in a nearby cottage, and Roosevelt had dismissed the two attendants who had transferred him from car to house. The hostess wondered how her guest would move from dining room to living room, but FDR said, "See me get to the next room!"

He pushed himself away from the dinner table and maneuvered himself to the floor. Then on hands and knees and without apparent self-consciousness, he crawled to the next room and lifted himself into a chair without assistance. He was immensely proud of his accomplishment and indicated that he now felt a new sense of security. Roosevelt had learned this method of movement because he had a dread of being caught alone and helpless in a fire.

During his stay in Massachusetts he learned to walk on canes and could get about with crutches and just one brace. However, though he never gave up hope that he would walk freely again, he never learned to walk entirely without braces.

His attention was finally shifted to a broken-down and decaying old southern resort in Warm Springs, Georgia, which contained a remarkable swimming pool. Roosevelt's friend, George Foster Peabody, a philanthropist and banker who owned the place, told him of its mineral pool and of its salutary effects on a young polio patient. When Roosevelt arrived in Georgia for the first time, he found a dilapidated pre-Civil War watering place with a shabby hotel that he labeled at a glance a "first-class firetrap."

One dip in the mineral-rich waters of the one-hundred-and-fifty-foot pool had such a therapeutic effect on him that he felt better than he had in years. The pool was fed from a subterranean spring, which gushed to the surface at an 88-degree temperature, its water rich with minerals and so buoyant that he could swim for two hours without fatigue.

FDR was thrilled with his immediate progress. The marvelous water started his toes tingling with "more life than I'd felt in them since August, 1921," he said. After a month of daily swimming he could walk in water 4 feet deep without braces or crutches almost as well as if he had nothing wrong with his legs.

The curative effects of the water caused his fertile mind to conjure up visions of a great center at Warm Springs for the cure of infantile paralysis. As his own hope soared, he felt more and more that this backward resort could be developed into a beautiful curative center, and he began to pour his energies and ideas into Warm Springs.

During the next few winters Roosevelt returned and drew up plans for a new pool, cottages, roads, and treatment areas. He gathered together the nucleus of a staff, including a doctor and physiotherapist to treat the growing group of patients drawn there by hopes of recovery.

He was so convinced of his dreams for Warm Springs that he took the big step of investing a considerable portion of his savings in its development, about two hundred thousand dollars. With his partner, Basil O'Connor, he set up a nonprofit institution, the Warm Springs Foundation, which was endorsed by the American Orthopedic Association as a hydrotherapeutic center, and its worth medically certified. Hard work, faith, and creative energy were bringing his dream to fruition, and Warm Springs became a second home to FDR.

He built his own cottage on 1,750 acres of land on nearby Pine Mountain, raised cattle there, and drove along the Pine Mountain Scenic Highway which he had taken great delight in designing. It was here in the gentle Georgia climate he loved, at the Little White House, that he died almost twenty years later.

Though his second home was in Georgia, his political base had always remained in New York. He had supported Al Smith's successful bid for governor again in 1926, and his years of loyal support for the governor reached completion in 1928, when Smith asked him to serve as floor manager at the Democratic convention in Houston.

There, speaking before a nationwide radio audience, FDR placed Smith's name in nomination for President. This time Smith won easily on the first ballot, and Roosevelt, fully aware of the power of the radio for the first time, won the confidence of millions of Americans with his intimate manner, clear speaking voice, and friendly charm.

Once nominated, Smith had to find a powerful figure to replace him as governor in influential New York State. As a Catholic, a Wet, and running against the popular Herbert Hoover, Smith was in trouble from the start. He needed Roosevelt for the glamorous name, upstate connections, middle-of-the-road position on Prohibition, and Protestant religion to help him win the critically important bloc of 47 electoral votes of New York State. There was only one difficulty. Roosevelt absolutely refused to run.

He and Louis Howe agreed that 1928 was not the year for him. Smith might very well be defeated and drag FDR down with him; he needed more time at Warm Springs to recuperate and to protect his financial stake in the center. All his arguments, however, did not persuade the desperate New York leaders. They clung to the hope that he would run, and Smith himself argued and cajoled and pleaded with Roosevelt to accept the nomination.

Roosevelt once again flatly declined, assuring Smith he could win the Presidency without him. Before the state convention began late in September, Roosevelt left for Warm Springs. Howe, who was absolutely opposed to his running, knew the pressures the party was exerting on his boss. "Beware of Greeks bearing gifts," he cautioned.

Smith did not give up. The second day of the convention he tried to get through to FDR by telephone, but Roosevelt refused to answer. Smith then contacted Eleanor who was attending the convention at Syracuse. He pleaded with her to persuade her husband to run. Eleanor insisted she would not influence him in any way but finally agreed to at least get him on the telephone.

FDR was delivering a speech for Smith at Manchester, Georgia, when word came to the speaker's platform that his wife was waiting on the phone. When he finished his speech, FDR went to the phone at the corner drugstore and laughingly told her he would not have answered for anyone but her. Eleanor said a hasty hello, handed the phone to Smith, and ran to catch a train. It was not until the next morning that she heard the results of that momentous conversation.

FDR again refused to run. But Smith assured him that Herbert Lehman, who was running for lieutenant governor, would assume much of the responsibility of office so that FDR could get away frequently. He promised financial support of Warm Springs by the chairman of the National Democratic Committee who was willing to pledge $25,000 to Roosevelt's center. He finally brought the argument down to a personal basis. Roosevelt must run, he said, if he wanted Smith to win the Presidency. The party needed him.

At that argument FDR hesitated, and the canny Smith must have sensed the momentary indecision. What would Roosevelt do, he asked, if his name were placed in nomination and he were drafted? Again FDR hesitated, for he did not know what he would do. Smith felt he had the advantage. He hung up and quickly set to work.

The next day Roosevelt was nominated for governor of New York by acclamation. Louis Howe was disgusted. "Mess is no name for it. For once I have no advice to give," he wired.

Eleanor sent the message, "Regret that you had to accept but know that you felt it obligatory."

When news of his nomination reached Warm Springs, general gloom set in. But characteristically,

Roosevelt led the way forward. "Well, if I've got to run for governor, there's no use in all of us getting sick about it!" he proclaimed.

He returned to New York and set about having the time of his life running for office. He literally thrived on the backbreaking schedule that followed for the next month. "If I could keep on campaigning twelve months longer, I'd throw away my canes," he exuberantly told a crowd.

The question of his poor health was the first one raised by Republicans after the nomination. Republican newspapers called him dangerously ill, perhaps risking his life to run. When reporters quizzed Al Smith on FDR's ability to do the job, Smith replied, "A governor does not have to be an acrobat. We do not elect him for his ability to do a double backflip or a handspring."

After a strenuous day of auto parades, seven speeches, and countless handshakes, Roosevelt's remarks on the subject brought a guffaw—"too bad about this unfortunate sick man, isn't it?"

He could almost be called an acrobat for his performance during the campaign, for he overcame the most difficult obstacles to speak everywhere. His piercing eyes, effortless smile, friendly handshake, and vigorous manner commanded attention wherever he traveled. With the aid of a competent staff, including Jim Farley and Sam Rosenman, later to be key aides when he became President, Roosevelt raised the issues of progressive government, aid to farmers, and development of public power.

First traveling by train and then by car, he stopped at every crossroads where prospective Democratic voters had gathered. His witty speeches and thoughtful opinions began to arouse the crowds, and they pushed into halls to hear FDR. Sometimes he had to be carried up fire escapes and through windows in order to speak to the people. When he reached an audience, he would adjust his braces, take his son Jimmy's arm, and walk out onto the platform smiling and make a joke about his physical condition. The crowd was put at ease and forgot his ailment.

On election night another test of courage came. It was evident after early returns that Al Smith would be buried in a Republican landslide in favor of Hoover. The gloom of defeat hung heavy in the air at the Hotel Biltmore. By midnight FDR's opponent, Albert Ottinger, moved so far ahead upstate that some morning papers were rolling off the presses announcing an Ottinger victory.

But Roosevelt insisted that the race for governor could be won by a very narrow margin. He feared that some counties were holding back returns and figured a bluff was necessary to prevent possible tampering with the ballot boxes. He and Ed Flynn got on the telephone and warned sheriff after sheriff in upstate counties that a staff of one hundred lawyers would be on the road the next morning to look for election fraud. This bold move may have swung the election in his favor.

Eleanor and Sara went to bed that night believing Roosevelt had lost, but when they awoke the next morning they were astonished to find that he was governor of New York. He had won by the tiny margin of 25,564 votes out of four and a quarter million. His entire political future had been shaped by a handful of Democratic voters who had created a new standard-bearer for their faltering party. Roosevelt had taken a giant step that would lead him to the White House.

CHAPTER NINE

★★★★★★

THE ROAD TO THE WHITE HOUSE

The crowds outside the Assembly chamber in Albany that first day of January, 1929, were somewhat silent and sad as they listened to the guns roar a salute to their new governor. Al Smith had been the state's most popular leader in history, and it would be hard for FDR to replace him in the people's affections.

Inside the brightly decorated chamber Roosevelt felt a moment of great triumph as he readied himself to speak before the assembled group of legislators and friends. Showing clearly in his poised manner was a confidence that he had conquered a debilitating illness and was on his way to achieving the heights that people were beginning to predict as his destiny.

His voice rang out true and clear. This would be an "era of good feeling," he assured the legislators. As the Republican majority listened attentively to his words, he pledged his administration to achieving a greater share of the good life for the state's citizens.

Searching for an issue to make his own, he had realized that the subject of public utilities and the use of power resources were of overriding interest to the people. In this inaugural address he served notice of his intent to concentrate on the problem. "In the brief time that I have been speaking to you there has run to waste on their paths toward the sea enough power from our rivers to have turned the wheels of a thousand factories, to have lit a million farmers' homes. . . ." he said.

But the politicians were in no mood to give this Democratic star rising in their midst a push up the ladder of success without challenging him along the way. Al Smith heard this inaugural address with rising bitterness; he had already suggested to the new governor certain policies to pursue and the right people to appoint and consult. Though FDR had listened respectfully enough when Smith had suggested his own former advisers, he declined to follow the advice.

He told Smith that he had chosen his own man, Guernsey Cross, as secretary to the governor. "You know I need a great, big, strong man as secretary. I need someone whom I can lean on physically, if necessary, and I think it will be better, Al," he said, but the tension between the two men grew.

Smith began to realize that the man he had supported intended to run the state independently, and this moment signified the turning point of their political relations. FDR was the undisputed winner, the new kingpin of state politics, and the defeated Smith left Albany with the knowledge that things had changed now between them. Communication between the two ranking Democrats in the state ceased almost at once, and tension and near hostility grew until it would finally burst with a dramatic confrontation later at the national convention in 1932.

If Roosevelt had coolly settled one issue, he was walking into another more explosive one with his hostile legislature. He had labored to prepare a careful executive budget, but when he presented it to the legislature in April, the hoped-for era of good feeling collapsed in ruins.

He wrote to his son, "I am getting into a grand little fight with the Legislature and from now on, for five weeks, it will be a general row." He always relished a good fray and jumped into this one with confidence that he would win.

The battle for the control of the state budget hinged on the constitutional amendment the people had recently passed giving more power over finances to the governor and less to the legislature. The lawmakers could now only retain or strike out key items but could not add new items without the governor's approval. The Republicans, however, were determined to keep control of budgetary detail. They returned his budget amended, which they knew he would refuse to accept.

"Either the state must carry out the principles of the Executive Budget, which embody fifteen years of effort to place the affairs of the state on a modern efficient business basis, or we shall drift into a hopeless situation of divided responsibility for administration of executive functions," Roosevelt warned as he vetoed the bill.

This brought about an impasse and renewed the battle, but after some delay and maneuvering through the state courts, the governor's point of view was upheld. FDR's fight over control of the budget caused a political tug-of-war with the hostile legislature that lasted throughout his term in office.

By summer the governor and his family were comfortably settled in the old Victorian mansion in Albany, and FDR thrived on filling the governorship of the most populous state in the union. He was developing a program that would build his power and prestige as he rebuilt his party. He appointed a commission to investigate the power question, "Whether a public utility has the right to make any old profit that it can, or not, in other words, as to whether there is any real distinction between a public utility and a purely private business." He wanted and gained the support of the people in his public power campaign, for he strongly believed that electric power should be developed for the benefit of the consumer.

He fully intended to carry forward Smith's progressive work of aiding women and children, improving the lot of the working man, and aiding farmers. Realizing the importance of the women's vote, he had appointed Frances Perkins as chairman of his Industrial Board. She would work for FDR for many years and become a trusted adviser on labor matters when he became President.

Meanwhile, always adaptable and an innovator, he recognized the importance of the press to his future re-election. He planned ways to get his programs across to the voters by conceiving the idea of a publicity bureau to send out free information to newspapers on what his administration was doing. The upstate papers particularly reported a biased Republican viewpoint to the voters, FDR felt, and he knew how much he needed those upstate votes. The publicity bureau turned out to be an effective instrument that let the people know exactly how their legislators were voting on issues crucial to their welfare.

Instinctively, he seemed to realize the importance of the mass media long before other politicians. His party set up an hour-long radio show each month on a statewide hookup, and he got his message across in informal talks. These were the start of what would later become the "fireside chats," so important a part of his communication with the people when he became President.

A steady stream of politicians, advisers, legislators, and guests of all sorts poured through the governor's mansion contributing proposals and ideas over which the governor calmly presided. He and Eleanor entertained frequently, and they seemed to thrive on the gay, stimulating, and informative conversation of the nightly dinner table. Eleanor worked as a teacher and public speaker and she brought home people involved in her activities. The children romped through on their way to various schools. Everyone was offered cordial hospitality. Guests would be ushered to the upstairs sitting room to discuss their special area of interest with FDR. After an informal chat, during which Roosevelt would absorb a remarkable amount of knowledge, the guests would usually leave mesmerized by his sincerity and persuasiveness.

He usually formed an informal relationship with men and truly relished a good laugh, especially swapping yarns with political cronies. He once said to Frances Perkins that politicians would rather have a "nice jolly understanding" of their problems than lots of patronage. "A little patronage, a lot of pleasure, and public signs of friendship and prestige—that's what makes a political leader secure with his people and that is what he wants anyhow!" said FDR.

But the good times and gay spirits were nearing an

end. Momentous economic changes were about to occur that would call for a new direction in governmental leadership. FDR, like most people, did not recognize ominous signs of impending economic crisis evident to a few astute students of the economy by late summer of 1929.

As he cruised the canals of the Empire State on a barge that summer, getting acquainted with conditions in rural and upstate New York, Roosevelt had no inkling that the New Era was destined to crash that very fall, and that a disastrous and dismal decade of bitter depression would fall upon the land.

The stock market had pushed further and further upward in what one historian called the greatest orgy of speculation and overoptimism since 1720. Early in September it reached the highest point of all time. Businessmen were more optimistic than ever for good times to continue at this high plateau and paid scant attention to ominous warnings when stocks suffered minor setbacks during the next months.

The final week in October, 1929, was a week of sudden economic catastrophe for the nation. The break began on Wednesday, October 23, with a fantastic drop in the market that caused stocks to plummet downward while utter confusion prevailed among desperate stockholders. The next day, Black Thursday, was the Day of Panic. The frenzy to sell at any price caused total chaos on the floor of the stock exchange. The visitor's gallery was closed, as tickers fell hopelessly behind in recording wild transactions. Prices held over the weekend, but by the next Tuesday, when brokers frantically tried to extricate themselves from the wreckage, sixteen million shares changed hands by closing time. The Great Crash had occurred, and the Golden Era of prosperity was at an end.

A dismal upward spiral of unemployment began that in less than three years would cause twelve million people, about 25 per cent of the working force, to lose their jobs. Some of these would be forced to live in shanties built of tin or in unoccupied freight cars. They would line up in breadlines and soup kitchens to get a bite to eat, their savings gone and work impossible to find.

From the beginning of the crash, President Hoover had maintained an optimistic public attitude, refusing to recognize that forceful measures must be taken to stop the downward thrust of the economic forces. "The fundamental business of the country, that is production and distribution of commodities, is on a sound and prosperous basis," he said, and in January of 1930, announced cheerfully that the unemployment trend had already been reversed. He firmly believed that the economy was basically sound and that maintaining prices and spending would effect a recovery. He also felt that giving relief to the unemployed would destroy their character and undermine local responsibility for taking care of their own poor, even when public and private relief sources were dwindling almost to the vanishing point.

As the national picture changed from prosperity to depression, Roosevelt had to run for re-election. In his campaign he again showed acute perception of the power of mass communication. Although talking pictures were still new, he made a film, *The Roosevelt Record*, and showed it extensively throughout the state.

He had managed to steer clear of Tammany involvement despite Republican cries of scandal in corruption-ridden New York City, where Mayor Jimmy Walker was gallivanting around. Roosevelt had wisely played down the touchy issue of Prohibition, and had managed to emerge the winner when Hoover sent his Republican "big guns," the Secretary of State and Secretary of War, to discredit him in his state.

Because of his record, Roosevelt won again in 1930 with an unprecedented majority of 725,000 votes, even carrying solidly Republican territory upstate that had never been taken by a Democrat before. He had a clear mandate from the people and was now indisputably a figure of national interest. "The Democrats nominated their President yesterday: Franklin D. Roosevelt," Will Rogers said of the election.

But the Presidential nomination was a full two

years away, and the task at hand was to help the people cope with the Depression. FDR was a man of action, and the actions he took to lessen the effects of hard times clearly foreshadowed the concepts of the future New Deal.

During his second term as governor, the commission he had appointed reported its study of the feasibility of developing the Saint Lawrence River as a low-cost source of hydroelectric power. The commissioners endorsed state development of power and private distribution of power through a contract method. This made headline news, and across the country FDR was associated with a strong public-power policy.

Actually, only the U.S. government could negotiate a treaty with Canada concerning the Saint Lawrence power possibilities, and President Hoover was unwilling to discuss the issue. But Roosevelt, though he had not won a final settlement, focused public opinion upon himself as a champion of a public power and utility policy that would help the consumer. People everywhere were impressed with his strong stand on their behalf.

The time had also come to take action on unemployment relief. He conferred with Frances Perkins on growing unemployment and called for a commission to study remedies. He announced a governor's conference to consider possible solutions to this growing problem that concerned them all. He began to believe that the government had the duty to prevent distress and to promote the general welfare of all the people.

His message to the legislature in August of 1931 was significant, for it marked a clear statement of his later New Deal philosophy.

"Our government is not the master but the creature of the people. The duty of the State toward the citizens is the duty of the servant to its master. The people have created it; the people, by common consent, permit its continual existence. . . . One of the duties of the State is that of caring for those of its citizens who find themselves the victims of such adverse circumstance as makes them unable to obtain even the necessities for mere existence without the aid of others. . . ."

These were great words of inspiration to people hungry for a leader who understood their plight, and they began to look to this man whose compassion for the downtrodden led him to try to help them. He proposed the nation's first public money for unemployment, relief for old age security, improvements for housing, aid for farmers, prison reforms for New York, and programs for hospital building. These measures to aid the stricken were impressive when contrasted with President Hoover's feeling that charity was corrupting and that unemployment was

only a local responsibility. Here in FDR's progressive
state program lay the seeds of the New Deal waiting
to take root.

CHAPTER TEN

★ ★ ★ ★ ★ ★

CAMPAIGN FOR THE PRESIDENCY

For his birthday in January, 1930, Louis Howe gave his boss a joke gift, a Politician's Magic Set, guaranteed to perform miracles on recalcitrant politicians. There was some magic and some luck in FDR's political career that ultimately enabled him to pluck the Presidential rabbit out of a hat. But there was also much political genius, the know-how that came with years of practical experience. And there was finally faith, the enormous trust that FDR inspired in people.

Roosevelt realized even before his re-election as governor that the Depression had speeded up his political time table. He no longer thought in terms of 1936 as his year to run for President. It must be 1932.

Of course, he disclaimed any notion of running for President throughout his first term as governor. He knew that any announcement would surely concentrate forces against him that were now scattered. Only after 1930 did he openly begin to discuss his Presidential aspirations with his immediate staff. He finally threw his hat into the ring in January, 1932, in the primary election in North Dakota. Now the moment was ripe, and he sent out his top lieutenants, Howe and Jim Farley, to manage clubs and go on junkets to line up delegates in key states. He gathered together his famous group of professors, the "Brain Trust," to advise and assist him, and an organization came into being.

He faced trouble in his own state of New York. Al Smith had unexpectedly arisen again as the Tammany choice for President, and Smith formally announced his desire for the nomination in February. FDR needed two thirds of the delegates' votes at the convention to win. A conservative Smith bloc might hang on to more than one third of the votes and cause a deadlock, forcing the convention to choose a dark-horse candidate.

But the liberal Roosevelt bandwagon, meanwhile, picked up force. The Democrats were hungry for a victory at the polls, and they came forward from the South where Smith was still hated, from the West where radicals favored the liberal approach, from old Harvard acquaintances, influential Washington senators, and other diverse groups.

In early state contests, Roosevelt pulled ahead, yet did not take a decisive lead. But the campaign ground to a near-halt, first in Massachusetts where Smith won in the primary, and then disas-

trously in California. There Speaker of the House
John N. Garner from Texas came out the victor in
the primary. Garner held great power as the shrewd
leader of the Democrats in the House of Representatives.

So as the Democratic convention opened in Chicago June 27, 1932, it was clear that Roosevelt would
not win the first-ballot victory he had counted on.
Farley, hoping that last-minute persuasion would
win critical votes, was present everywhere, clapping
delegates on the back and urging them to jump on
the FDR bandwagon while there was still time.
Howe worked frantically behind the scenes to capture key favorite-sons' votes. Roosevelt sat near his
telephone in Albany ready to hear the news and confer on policy.

It was dawn before the first roll call of nominees
began. It brought the expected results: Roosevelt led
with 666¼ over runner-up Smith's 201¾. This was
not a two-thirds majority. Garner trailed with 90
votes and another favorite son captured 52 votes.
At this point Farley and Howe expected a stampede
for their man, but delegates were dead tired and beginning to stall.

On the next vote FDR picked up only 11½ votes,
and after a third roll call it became clear that no
stampede was in the making; that, quite to the con-
trary, one small breaking away could lead to full-
scale revolt on the next vote.

Time was critical if a deadlock was not to occur. Jim Farley and Joseph P. Kennedy, FDR supporter, wealthy financier, and father of a future President, called newspaper publisher William Randolph Hearst, who controlled the California delegation pledged to Garner. Hearst hated Smith and Newton D. Baker, Wilson's Secretary of War, who was another dark-horse possibility. Hearst was persuaded to switch to Roosevelt, and "Cactus Jack" Garner was offered the Vice-Presidency in exchange for his Texas votes.

Now that Texas had come around, on the fourth ballot an avalanche of votes rolled in. First McAdoo of California, himself an expert in the business of winning nominations, came to the platform. "California came here to nominate a President of the United States . . . . California casts 44 votes for Franklin D. Roosevelt," he cried above the shouts of Smith supporters. Others followed suit.

When the roll call was complete, 945 votes had been counted for Roosevelt. Ironically, it was only the bitter delegation of the "Happy Warrior" that had refused to make the nomination unanimous.

FDR had the nomination as the Democratic candidate for President.

The winner realized intuitively that the nation, bewildered, dismayed, and depressed as it was, would welcome a bold and daring move. So he thought of one that would show just what kind of man he was. With his superb sense of showmanship, he decided to rush to the airport and fly to Chicago to accept the nomination. It was unheard of for a politician to fly in a plane, and to accept the nomination in person was a complete break with tradition as well.

He hurried the family aboard a new trimotored plane in Albany, and they all had a bumpy and uncomfortable flight across country. In Chicago the band played "Happy Days Are Here Again" over and over and the delegates waited for their nominee to appear.

He came from the airport in a big white car, and in strong, eloquent words accepted their nomination. "I pledge you, I pledge myself, to a new deal for the American people," he told the cheering throng. Little did he realize that he had just named an era, for "New Deal" caught the fancy of the people and stuck in their minds as a fresh term for the better times that he promised.

Then the campaign began, and it was carefully planned. FDR's advisers told him that the battle was already won, that he could sit and rock on his front porch and still win an overwhelming victory. They told him the Republicans had lost the confidence of the people and that President Hoover had no chance of winning.

But Roosevelt had different ideas. He loved campaigning, circulating among the people, listening to their complaints, joking and smiling, and letting them see him in radiant good health. He felt it was vital to show himself as strong and vigorous to the people to dispel all notions of illness. And this he accomplished. He traveled 27,000 miles back and forth across the country, and in between junkets he spoke on a national radio network. Everywhere he went the crowds were mesmerized by his glorious smile, energetic manner, and eloquent speech.

Speaking from the rear platforms of trains and in meeting halls, he got across his message that the party could do something for the nation to replace the depressed economy with a New Deal for the "forgotten man at the bottom of the economic pyramid." Although his programs for reform covered a wide range of ideas, it was primarily a campaign of personalities and moods. The contrast between the self-confident man of action and the rigid, bitter White House incumbent was overwhelmingly clear.

President Hoover, grim and determined yet certain of defeat, continued to defend his Administration in long, dull speeches. He angrily called FDR a "chameleon on plaid," charging that Roosevelt changed his political viewpoint according to whom he was speaking.

During the course of the campaign, FDR perfected the programs he planned to initiate if elected. These were based on the idea that the government must regulate economic power for the common good, that everyone had a right to a good living, and that industry and agriculture would produce enough goods to spare.

He continued to criticize Hoover until the end, when he went home to Hyde Park to vote. Election night he arrived at the Biltmore Hotel in New York City. This was the most critical, the most important night of his life, one that he had worked for years to see. And before the night was through, the work of a lifetime was rewarded. Franklin Delano Roosevelt became the next President of the United States. He won an overwhelming victory and took every state of the union but six. He won a clear majority. His total vote was close to twenty-three million to Hoover's slightly less than sixteen million.

The aristocrat from Hyde Park had been chosen by the people to guide them out of the crisis and toward a better life. After all the excitement had died down, and Roosevelt was alone, he sat soberly thinking of the monumental responsibility that had been placed upon him.

This was November, but the new President could not actually take over the reins of government until March 4, 1933. He was the last President to have to suffer through such a long wait, for Congress in a few months would ratify a change to call for inauguration of the President in January instead of March.

In the long interim that year, while the country

waited for the new President to take office, an incident occurred in Florida that ended in near catastrophe. As FDR toured Miami, a short, dark man named Zangara suddenly leaped out of the crowd and began to fire shot after shot at the President-elect. Luckily he missed his target, but he did hit people in the crowd and fatally wounded the mayor of Chicago, who was a member of Roosevelt's party.

This attempted assassination sharpened the feeling of crisis that gripped the people that winter. Banks across the country faltered in the economic crisis and by February five thousand banks had shut their doors. This was the first problem FDR would have to face after he took the oath of office.

On Inauguration Day, March 4, 1933, a cold wind blew through the chilled crowds that assembled under a cloudy sky to see the new President take over. Solemnly, he repeated the oath of office. Now he was the thirty-second President of the United States, and in a grave voice said simply to the nation, ". . . let me assert my firm belief that the only thing we have to fear is fear itself. . . ." He promised action, and closed his talk, "May God guide me in the days to come."

Once in the White House, his wife described the inaugural ceremony. "It was very, very solemn, and a little terrifying. . . . The crowds were so tremendous, and you felt that they would do anything—if only someone would tell them what to do."

That day Eleanor began her long reign as the First Lady of the land, and FDR plunged into action as he had promised. The people had registered a desire for direct, vigorous leadership, and the new President, calm and serene as he faced the greatest crisis he had known, set forth to lead the people forward to better times.

CHAPTER ELEVEN

★ ★ ★ ★ ★

THE FIRST NEW DEAL

FDR awoke his first morning in the White House unaccustomed to the blank walls of the bedroom and the set of newspapers that lay at his bedside. After breakfast, he went to the Oval Room where his Presidential office would be and gazed at the blank surface of his desk. He could find no pencil or paper in the empty drawers, not even a buzzer to ring for a secretary.

Not a soul seemed to be around to assist him, and this was no way to get things done. Suddenly the President leaned back in his chair, opened his mouth wide, and let out a huge yell. Secretaries, aides, staff, all came running. The President had called for action, and the momentum of the First Hundred Days was about to begin.

He had already chosen his Cabinet officers, and they had turned their attention first to the banking crisis. Two measures were already prepared to deal with the crisis, since many banks throughout the country had already collapsed financially. The first measure the President took was the drastic step of declaring a bank holiday, closing the doors of every bank in the nation. His plan was to reopen them gradually on a sounder basis.

This shocked and bewildered the people whose savings were already dwindling and now were locked away completely. The President knew he had to explain this action to the people to restore their confidence in the banking community, so he went before the public in his first radio fireside chat. In warm and simple terms he explained just how he would deal with the banks. He then called Congress into special session and proposed his Emergency Banking Act to open banks under an orderly and licensed system.

His talk on the radio and his direct action with Congress generated a fresh mood of hope among the people. Some called it a wave of sunlight, for now citizens knew that bold action would be used to renew the country.

FDR sensed the mood of the people and Congress. He had them on his side, and now was the time to move ahead to enact the new laws that were needed. So in the next hundred days he pushed through a torrent of important bills to set forces moving toward recovery.

With public opinion solidly behind him, he warned Congress that the national crisis called for emergency measures and the bills poured forth. First came an Economy Bill to cut government costs and balance the federal budget as he had promised to do if elected. Then other proposals and plans followed in rapid order. In one hundred days he made ten speeches, sent Congress fifteen messages, pushed through many laws, talked to reporters at twice-weekly press conferences, and conferred constantly with influential men. Through all the hard work he displayed a remarkable brand of confidence and good cheer that amazed all who worked with him.

These were the bills that he handed to Congress those First Hundred Days:

March	*9*	*Emergency Banking Act*
March	*20*	*Economy Act*
March	*31*	*Civilian Conservation Corps*
April	*19*	*Gold Standard abandoned (ratified June 5)*
May	*12*	*Federal Emergency Relief Act*
		Agricultural Adjustment Act
		Emergency Farm Mortgage Act
May	*18*	*Tennessee Valley Authority Act*
May	*27*	*Truth-in-Securities Act*
June	*13*	*Home Owner's Loan Act*
June	*16*	*National Industrial Recovery Act*
		Glass–Steagall Banking Act
		Farm Credit Act

Just after the President's inauguration, Will Rogers had said, "America hasn't been as happy in three years as they are today. No money, no banks, no work, no nothing, but they know they got a man in there who is wise to Congress, wise to our so-called big men. The whole country is with him." The people felt that FDR's New Deal was trying to deal a new deck of cards that would not be stacked against them.

FDR liked and knew how to work with people. At the beginning of his term a ragged army of poor and hungry veterans of World War I marched on Washington to demand money for their Army service. They had done the same when Hoover was President, and Hoover had called out the Army to disband their camp and burn down their tents. When they marched on Roosevelt, he promptly sent doctors, food, coffee, tents, the Navy band to play for them, and his wife to talk with them. Eleanor marched through the mud of their camp and sang songs with them.

"Hoover sent the Army; Roosevelt sent his wife," they all said, and most of them joined the Civilian Conservation Corps or went home. This was the emotion he inspired.

His Civilian Conservation Corps pulled young men off the streets and gave them jobs that would help build up the country. By June of that year, camps all over the country housed young men who worked to plant forests, construct dams, or build parks. The health and morale of these boys improved quickly, although they had not eaten well or lived decently for some time. Part of their wages were sent home to families, and by the coming of winter, fewer people had the same dread of cold and hunger that many had felt the year before.

The Federal Emergency Relief Act provided five hundred million dollars to improve roads, build schools, airports, parks, and sewer systems. FDR saw to it that money found its way directly to the people so they could buy food and clothes and earn self-respect by working again. Money was spent on reforestation, flood control, water works, sewage plants, and slum clearance. Artists, musicians, writers, and white-collar workers were hired to write histories of their communities, paint murals for post offices, and catalog libraries. A federal theater project employed actors and writers to write and produce plays. Gradually, people gained new hope and purpose as Roosevelt's New Deal took hold.

The President created an even grander scheme to join business and government for the common good. New Dealers felt that if every factory, shop, and business voluntarily agreed to draw up codes of fair practice, regulate wages and work hours, forbid child labor, and agree to enforce such codes, the economy would benefit. So the National Industrial Recovery Act was born, and soon its symbol, a blue eagle clutching a cogwheel, and the slogan "We Do Our Part," was plastered on store windows and on the products of some seven hundred industries that joined the National Recovery Administration (NRA). The President had great hopes for his plan.

Later the NRA would be declared unconstitutional, but before it was outlawed it made progress in improving living and working conditions. It got rid of many sweatshops, removed many young children from miserable toil in factories, helped organized labor get a bigger share of what it produced, and induced people to think more in terms of national planning and cooperation between business and labor.

The plight of the farmer was almost worse than that of the factory worker. Farmers were earning so little money they could not afford even the rock-bottom prices of consumer products. Bread cost five cents a loaf, tomatoes eight pounds for five cents, lettuce a penny a pound, sliced bacon ten cents a pound, and sirloin steak twenty cents a pound, but hardly any farmer was able to afford even these prices.

Sharecroppers of the South who rented a bit of land from a large landowner lived in misery. And the disaster of drought in the early 1930's brought a dust bowl to the prairie states, with soil parched and cracked until the wind blew choking black clouds across the dry earth. The helpless farmer watched his crops wither away and his cattle die for lack of water.

The farmers had made so little money on their crops that they could not make payments on their farms. But men who had worked land for years refused to give up their property and stood in their barnyards, shotgun in hand, to ward off any foreclouser who came to demand payment. The President knew that violence could break out at any time, and he halted the foreclosing of mortgages and gave the farmers loans to preserve their farms.

The President had wanted to help farmers before planting season and had immediately proposed the Agricultural Adjustment Act, but it took two months to get the bill through Congress. By then cotton was already planted and a huge supply of baby pigs was on hand. The President's bill reduced planting of staple products like wheat, cotton, and tobacco, and cut down on breeding of pigs and cattle so that prices would go up. Ten million acres of cotton already growing in the fields were plowed under, and farmers were paid for it. Six million piglets were purchased from farmers to be given to families on relief. The idea of subsidy was to pay farmers to cut production so that prices would rise and prosperity return.

Slowly, the Agriculture Adjustment Act measures helped to raise overall farm income, and the AAA eventually turned out to be one of the most successful and popular measures of the New Deal.

The President also tried to find ways to improve

America's financial system. He took the country off the gold standard, stabilized the gold content of the dollar at about half its former value, and brought reforms to the stock exchange and banks to prevent another crash. Federal insurance for banks meant that savings could not be wiped out by economic depressions or crashes. This increased the people's faith in the reopened banks and began to stabilize the financial community.

Perhaps one of the greatest achievements of the First Hundred Days was the law passed to create the Tennessee Valley Authority. This law brought to reality a dream of abundance and well-being for several million people who had been living in poverty. The plan was to control a mighty river through a system of dams. The work took twenty years, but it changed the 652-mile-long Tennessee River from an annual monster of flood and destruction to a peaceful and useful source of water and power for an enormous valley.

Ultimately, the TVA brought cheap and plentiful electricity, inland waterways for better transportation, and nitrate plants that produced inexpensive fertilizer for farmers. By using powerful water resources more wisely, an entire valley three-fourths the size of England benefited from cooperation and planning, its people learned better farming techniques, and rose out of a life of poverty to abundance on their now fertile land.

Measures such as TVA and CCC were examples of FDR's dreams of conserving the resources of the country. Other laws provided for planting forests in huge areas of otherwise useless land, protecting public rangelands, and building great dams such as Boulder Dam on the Colorado River, Grand Coulee Dam on the Columbia, and the Bonneville Dam in Oregon.

Altogether, the First Hundred Days of Roosevelt's Administration were as exciting and productive as any in the history of the nation. The measures passed during that period started a chain of legislation and action that significantly changed the course of American life in the twentieth century. For the first two years of his term Roosevelt rode a great wave of popularity. And when Congressional election time came in 1934, the people responded by giving Roosevelt's Democrats an even greater majority in both Houses of Congress.

But as with all popular administrations, the honeymoon did not last forever. After 1934 there were increasing signs of resistance to the President. Business began to turn away from him, and FDR looked instead to farmers, laborers, and poor people as a base of support.

Of course, the measures passed during the first years of the New Deal did not immediately solve all the problems of the Depression. Consumer buying power did not rise fast enough. Businessmen did not fully cooperate on regulating prices. Employers continued to cut wages as they saw fit.

Some of the New Deal organizations, which had been born in a frenzy of activity, slowly lost steam. Within two years of its birth, the NRA, for instance, was in trouble. It had not fulfilled all its promises, and it was attacked as an illegal body. In 1935, the Supreme Court, with conservative justices in the majority, heard a case brought against the NRA and declared the whole act unconstitutional.

Newspapers became more critical of FDR policies, and cartoons showed him as a diabolical leader. Roosevelt realized that he could not change the ill will of the press, but he always kept the channels of communication open, and reporters enjoyed the easy jokes and light touch of his press conferences even though their publishers attacked the President. FDR wisely recognized how important it was to keep the people informed and continued his regular and friendly talks over the radio.

Demagogues of the political right and left began to shout loud and bitter words against the President. Politicians with great ambitions and men with crackpot schemes held out to the people all sorts of fantastic plans and promises. Communists and Fascists joined in the criticism, and the thunder of voices from the left and right began to unnerve some New Deal leaders.

But quietly and courageously the President ignored criticism and kept his own counsel, picking his way among the pressures from both sides. Confidently he reshaped his policies to steal his critics' thunder. FDR always preferred to combine alternative ideals in shaping a plan. He told reporters he was like a quarterback in a football game. He could not say what the play after next was going to be until the next play was completed. "If the play makes ten yards, the succeeding play will be different from what it would have been if they had been thrown for a loss. I think that is the easiest way to explain it," he said of his way of working.

Meanwhile, he always kept an ear attuned to public opinion. He listened carefully to Eleanor when she reported the situation of the people after one of her frequent fact-finding trips. "Look at the condition of their clothes on the wash line . . . notice their cars," he told her, and he would always ask what people were eating, how they lived, and what their farms looked like.

By 1935 increased pressures from the left forced him to join more closely with the progressive elements of the party and with a Congress that passed the Wagner Bill to give greater power to labor. One of the most important bills of the New Deal went through Congress in 1935. This was the Social Security Act to give greater aid to the aged and help the unemployed, blind, and crippled, and dependent mothers and children.

But as FDR and Congress moved toward the left, the nine men who sat as judges on the United States Supreme Court were moving in the opposite direction. In 1935 they considered a host of cases to decide if it was constitutional for the federal government to wield the great power FDR had used in passing New Deal laws. The court decided that some of this federal power was unconstitutional and that Congress could not give the President such authority. Although many New Deal measures were held to be legal, the Supreme Court ruled that some were not. The court not only declared the NRA unconstitutional, but it also found the Agricultural Adjustment Act an invasion of states' rights.

These Supreme Court decisions angered Roosevelt deeply, for he saw them as a grave threat to his New Deal achievements. But the 1936 election was approaching, and he held his temper for the time being. After he was re-elected he would deal with the nine "old men" of the Supreme Court—and unfortunately it would be in a way that would leave a scar on his Administration.

CHAPTER TWELVE

★ ★ ★ ★ ★ ★

FROM SUCCESS TO FAILURE

On the evening of his nomination for a second term, FDR made his way slowly through the mobs of cheering delegates on the convention floor. Smiling around at the sea of friendly faces, his sharp eye spotted the distinguished poet Edwin Markham in the crowd. Markham had written a poem honoring the "forgotten man," called "The Man With the Hoe," which was a favorite of the President's.

He smiled and stopped to greet the white-maned poet. Markham leaned forward across the crowd to shake hands with the President, but he was shoved by people who wanted a closer glimpse of FDR. The poet fell heavily against the President's son, who supported his father by the arm. Suddenly Roosevelt felt his leg brace give way, and he swayed and toppled helplessly. Horrified, a Secret Service agent dived forward and caught him just as he hit the floor.

"Clean me up," the shaken President ordered and searched around for pages of the speech he had dropped. The episode was symbolic of the precarious position in which FDR would be during most of his second term in the White House. But here at the national Democratic convention, at the end of his first four successful years in office, the President quickly regained his composure and continued toward the rostrum to accept the nomination for President.

Before the enthusiastic gathering that evening, he delivered a speech that some called the greatest they had ever heard. In strong and confident terms he said, "I cannot with candor tell you that all is well with the world. . . . Clouds of suspicion, tides of ill will and intolerance gather darkly in many places. . . ." But he added, "This generation of Americans has a rendezvous with destiny."

He then set out on a cross-country campaign to fulfill his own rendezvous with destiny. There was no doubt across the nation that he would win. His place in the people's hearts was a special one, and everywhere he went crowds showed evidence of their enthusiasm and support.

On election night in Hyde Park he heard the predicted results. Roosevelt's victory was an overwhelming affirmation of his Presidency. He had received the largest Presidential vote in history. Throughout the country, farmers, union men, Negroes, the poor, all had voted Democratic. He was re-elected by 24,477,000 votes to 16,680,000 for his Republican opponent Alf Landon. He had won all the electoral votes of every single state in the union except Maine and Vermont.

In the midst of the jubilation, everyone called him a master politician; his political reputation soared to its zenith. But the President must have had a few fleeting moments of concern. The top-heavy majority of Democrats in Congress that came in on his coat-tails might spell trouble for him. He knew well that conservative and liberal factions might split the party and in their battles abandon his New Deal programs. Unfortunately, this did occur, and before long FDR's great election victory was turned to ashes.

A few said the famous Roosevelt luck started to change when a dark and somber sky covered Washington on Inauguration Day. He faced Chief Justice Hughes on the gray and gloomy day in January, 1937. As he took the oath of office for President, he faced the adversary he secretly intended to tackle first in his new Administration.

But now he spoke out simply and seriously to the nation.

"I see one-third of a nation ill-housed, ill-clad, ill-nourished," he said, and he vowed to lead the people forward. Behind the speech was the sure knowledge that to be able to move forward he must first hurdle the obstacle of a Supreme Court that had grown old. He felt most of the justices lived in a "horse-and-buggy" age, one antagonistic to his goals and those of his New Deal.

For some time he had grappled with the problem of what to do with this group of "nine old men," the judges of the highest court in the land. He felt he had to bring them into line, for they had declared unconstitutional some of his most important New Deal legislation. The President was extremely bitter over their recent decisions against his program and believed they had created an impossible situation where neither the federal nor state governments could pass needed laws.

In secrecy, without the benefit of advice from his closest staff, he developed a plan to change the makeup of the court to ensure that it would be a more liberal body. He proposed to appoint a new justice for every justice who failed to retire after the age of seventy—six out of the nine judges were already over seventy years old. Eventually six more judges might sit on the court on an equal basis to decide critical issues. The President's argument was that the justices were overworked and needed assistance.

Shortly after he was sworn in, the President made his plan public. But without any advance warning to his Cabinet, the Congress, or the nation, the proposal dropped like a bombshell. The people were shocked and distressed over FDR's secrecy and dictatorial way of approaching the problem. Across the nation citizens watched the battle develop between Congress and the President, and they flooded their Representatives with mail opposing Roosevelt's court-packing scheme. Battle lines formed, mail piled high on Capitol Hill desks, and the most bitter fight of the New Deal raged.

Roosevelt confidently thought the people were with him, but for once his political instinct failed. Neither the people nor his own advisers or Cabinet could support the President in his plan to change the makeup of the court. He fought for six long months, trying to get his proposal passed by Congress. But he lost. The House and Senate refused to change the traditional composition of the Supreme Court and defeated Roosevelt's bill.

His enemies had a field day, thinking that Roosevelt's great magic was gone, but they failed to recognize that, while he had lost the battle, he had won the war. Gradually, the court's decisions had begun to take a more liberal turn, and the justices began to sustain laws favorable to his New Deal. One of the justices retired, and Roosevelt was able to appoint Senator Hugo Black to the bench, thereby tipping the balance toward the liberal wing. The court fight was over. But in the long run, the President had lost prestige and stature in the fight, and this was only a portent of things to come.

The Supreme Court fight demonstrated the independence of the new Congress, and the next two years were difficult ones during which FDR had little legislative control. He constantly had to deal with a conservative coalition of Democrats and Republicans who sought to block his actions at every turn. The Supreme Court decision had marked an end to Congressional support of FDR and his first New Deal.

Although most of his New Deal legislation had already become law, including the recent Wagner Bill to aid in labor problems and a far-reaching Social Security measure, FDR realized that he must seek a new course of action that would be based less on federal intervention and more on free enterprise and competition.

He took a short jaunt around the country after re-election and proudly saw evidence everywhere of the good the New Deal was doing for the country. Huge dams held back rampaging waters while parks and grazing lands were being created. Industry was set for increased production, and people were back on the job. He felt great pride, and everywhere people shared his hopefulness. "He saved my family. He gave me a job," people said to his staff.

But when he returned to Washington, he was almost stunned at the difference in atmosphere. Men who had been elected to office using his golden name for support now refused to cooperate with him. Even though he was their party's leader, he could wield little influence or control.

He had come to rely on a new coalition of Democrats, depending upon city dwellers, ethnic groups, and especially labor for his support. Under his protective Administration labor unions had grown and organized rapidly. But with increased union power had come unrest and rivalries, and by the mid-thirties, bloody strikes. Tension and violence between rival unions and between companies and unions mounted. Sit-down strikes hit General Motors; blood was spilled in a great steel strike.

Middle-class Americans looked with horror at the fights and violence. They blamed the unions and the New Deal for encouraging the unions. As unions grew more powerful, the middle classes began to desert the New Deal and return to the Republican party. Big business attacked the President more than ever.

Added to the loss of prestige from the court defeat and labor unrest was new trouble in the economy. In the fall of 1937, a recession suddenly occurred. It scared the nation. Recovery had been moving along smoothly when a wave of selling hit the stock market, causing rising unemployment and a dropping economy. Anxious citizens got panicky and demanded action, but FDR remained optimistic and waited for an upswing in the spring.

His enemies taunted him for slowness, and his advisers pleaded for action. When matters did not improve, some urged him to rely on a balanced budget while others insisted that heavy spending was the only solution.

In the spring of 1938 he decided to move in favor of the philosophy of British economist John Maynard Keynes. His theory called for deliberate heavy public spending, called deficit spending, to stimulate the economy in times of recession. Several weeks after the President's order to start deficit spending, Congress passed a three-billion-dollar program and the economy began to move upward.

Although Roosevelt's popularity had declined and many in Congress shouted words of opposition, the second New Deal actually produced much good. Public works on dams, hospitals, and schools were continued, projects to help slum dwellers were started, an anti-monopoly program was launched, another in soil conservation and surplus food storing was begun, workers' wages were raised, and employment of young children was outlawed completely.

By the spring of 1938, however, the growing conservative coalition of Southern Democrats and Republicans was a real problem. Especially distrustful of his power, the conservatives were more determined than ever to block him. Allied with the conservatives were the nation's newspaper publishers whose editorials gave the President much criticism and little support.

People, afraid of his power and watching the horrifying example of Hitler in Germany, called him a power-mad dictator, and his opponents fanned these fears. He suffered defeat in Congress when he tried to modernize the executive management of government. When he tried to calm the people's fears, his opponents whispered, "The old Roosevelt magic has lost its kick."

He finally decided it was time to act. He had to get rid of the anti-Roosevelt Democrats in the fall election of 1938. So he set out on a stumping tour across the nation to purge the party. He used his persuasive personality to let the people know just where their local congressmen stood, honestly and frankly, sometimes having to speak out bitterly and sadly against old friends who had not upheld his principles. He honestly believed that this exposé of "false" Democrats was vital for the welfare of the people.

But the Roosevelt purge did not succeed. "It's a bust," said his friends with one look at election results. In state after state men who had become opposed to New Deal policies were re-elected, and the President fell to the lowest point of all time in his Presidency that winter. An anti-Roosevelt Congress now had the upper hand and was on the march.

The New Deal had reached the end of its crusade. It had helped the forgotten man to rise, but now it was over, and the nation began a swing toward the right. Yet other momentous events were happening all the while in the world, ominous acts that began to crowd out domestic issues.

Increasingly, Roosevelt was forced to turn his attention away from Congressional difficulties and face outward to the spiraling problems of world diplomacy. From now on, foreign affairs would absorb Roosevelt, for a grave world crisis had gradually developed that was beginning to threaten the country's very existence.

CHAPTER THIRTEEN

★ ★ ★ ★ ★ ★

INVOLVEMENT IN WORLD AFFAIRS

The week that Roosevelt had first become President of the United States in March, 1933, an ominous shadow had appeared across the world horizon. That week, in the last free elections in the German nation, Hitler and his Nazi storm troopers were voted into power. That week Japanese soldiers occupied Jehol, the capital city of a province of China. The insidious threat of world war had begun to spread.

A few people could see it coming, and President Roosevelt was one of those. But through the decade of the thirties, most people would watch the march of fascism cross Europe and Asia and turn their eyes away, hoping that America would keep out of a foreign war.

Though Roosevelt was a strong leader, he had to remain flexible in world affairs. He soon foresaw that the Nazi menace could lead to a reign of terror across Europe that would threaten world peace, and he would have preferred to stand up to Hitler and stop fascist ambitions at once. But Congress was controlled by hard-line isolationists, and they absolutely refused to take part in any international wars. The average American agreed.

In his first term, FDR concentrated on building a solid foundation for the domestic economy, leaving little time for foreign affairs. He did appoint an internationalist Secretary of State, Cordell Hull, who concluded reciprocal agreements to free the flow of international trade and to lower tariffs on certain products.

Roosevelt also took the big step of reversing U.S. policy toward the Soviet Union. During the twenties and early thirties the government had not recognized communist Russia. But by 1933 people felt that a potential trade market with Russia was being neglected by nonrecognition, and Roosevelt agreed. The Russians made solemn promises to settle American claims on property lost during the Revolution, which Roosevelt believed. He felt too that by recognizing that nation, he could create a buffer to Japanese and German expansion. But after the United States began diplomatic relations with the communist nation, trade did not reach the expected level, the Communists did not cease efforts to build the party in America as they had promised, and relations between the two countries remained cool.

A friendly policy toward nations of Latin America was most important in FDR's efforts in foreign diplomacy, and he encouraged a Good Neighbor relationship that grew over the years. He renounced traditional policies of armed intervention and interference in the politics of Latin American countries and withdrew marines who were still stationed in Haiti. The ideal of mutual defense grew throughout the western hemisphere as Europe drew closer to war, and FDR eventually negotiated mutual defense pacts for the protection of North and South America.

Meanwhile, as he struggled with domestic issues, he watched with horror the German persecution of Jews and other minority groups and continued his moral persuasion to bring about disarmament. His hopes, however, were dashed as Hitler's armies grew and Japan marched deeper into Manchuria.

Unfortunately, the President's hands were tied in foreign affairs, especially after Republican Senator Nye in 1935 started a Senate committee investigation of the World War I armaments industry. The committee's purpose, some felt, was to discredit President Wilson's Democratic Administration, declaring that armament-makers and bankers had made huge profits on the war. The committee succeeded in convincing many people that World War I had been a mistake and that Americans must stay at peace at all costs. To avoid war from occurring ever again, Congress passed the Neutrality Act of 1935.

This act provided that war supplies could not be sold either to aggressor or victim in time of conflict.

It specified a warning to American citizens that they could travel on ships of belligerents only at their own risk and prevented American ships from carrying munitions to nations at war. Since Congress wanted no part of war, the legislators felt that this Neutrality Act would keep the President from helping any nation in time of war.

Benito Mussolini, the Italian fascist leader, and Adolf Hitler, the Nazi dictator, were delighted. The Americans had proclaimed they would not take sides in a crisis, and the Fascists and Nazis prepared their tanks and guns and armies to march undisturbed across Europe. Over the next few years a relentless program of terror, propaganda, and conquest would bring them to the brink of world domination.

Ethiopia became the first victim of fascist aggression. In 1935 Italian troops invaded Ethiopia and the Neutrality Act forced FDR to stand by helplessly. He wanted to send help to Ethiopia but could not do so. He had to impose embargoes on arms to either side and warn businessmen not to trade with either side. With the taking of Ethiopia, Mussolini joined hands with Hitler to form the Rome–Berlin Axis.

The black specter of war cast an even greater pall across the European continent the summer of 1936. In the heat of July civil war broke out in Spain. General Francisco Franco's Falangists (fascists) revolted against the republican government and attempted to take the country by force. The fighting cruelly devastated the land and people of Spain, for Hitler and Mussolini cleverly realized this war could be a perfect staging ground to test their growing military machine. They poured soldiers and airplanes into Spain to destroy defenseless towns.

France and Great Britain feared Adolf Hitler's wrath if they should send aid to the loyalist side. They agreed to keep out, to send no aid to either side, hoping optimistically that this action would localize the war and keep it from spreading outside of Spain.

For some Americans, the Spanish Civil War was a crucial event. They realized that it foretold the coming struggle between the forces of democracy and fascism; some volunteered to fight with the loyalists, and some lost their lives on Spanish battlegrounds. The unhappy Roosevelt tried to cooperate with the Spanish government. But he could give them no help and with growing anger he watched the continuous stream of fascist aid pouring into Spain while the democracies stood by.

A month after the outbreak of the Spanish war FDR talked to the American people and repeated what they all felt. "We shun political commitments which might entangle us in foreign wars. . . . I hate war," he said.

But his heart ached as he watched fascism begin its steady march of destruction across the lands of Europe. He pleaded with and cajoled Congressional leaders to give him a freer hand, to let him help victims of aggression by applying embargoes against attacking nations. But stubborn isolationists blocked him and renewed the Neutrality Act once again in 1937. FDR could only offer strong words and moral encouragement.

He tried to stimulate more concern for international issues. In a speech in Chicago in October, 1937, called his Quarantine Speech, he warned Americans that if aggression triumphed elsewhere in the world, Americans could expect no mercy. "When an epidemic of physical disease starts to spread, the community approves and joins in a quarantine of the patients in order to protect the health of the community against the spread of the disease." He proposed a quarantine of the aggressors, speaking out more strongly on foreign policy than any President had for sixteen years.

The American people did not want to hear such a speech. Isolationist congressmen and pacifists reacted violently. They threatened the President with impeachment. Newspaper editorials shouted, "Stop Foreign Meddling; America Wants Peace."

FDR tried to get the people to face the truth. "It's a terrible thing to look over your shoulder when you are trying to lead—and find no one there," he said. And while Congress continued to bury its head in the sands of isolation, dictators consolidated their gains. In the fall of 1937 they formed the Axis alliance between Germany, Italy, and Japan.

Japanese military leaders had watched intently the preoccupation of the United States with European diplomacy. They had conquered Manchuria in 1931 and ordered armies to march deeper into northern China itself. Striking more boldly, they bombed an American gunboat anchored on the Yangtze River and knew FDR could do little more than protest. They attacked Shanghai and inflicted heavy damage on the city. Within a year they would control almost all of eastern China, while the United States, in an agony of indecision, continued to supply them with the gasoline and high-grade iron and scrap steel to build their war machine.

Meanwhile, the Axis leader, Hitler, spread his visions of conquest and glory to the German people. By March of 1938 his army was poised to march across Europe. He proclaimed union with Austria, and German soldiers goose-stepped across the Austrian border and over the cobblestone streets of Vienna. Next he looked eastward to Czechoslovakia, where three million Sudeten Germans had demanded independence from Prague. As Americans wondered what he would do, Hitler struck. He demanded "justice" for Sudetenland, and simply laughed when FDR denounced his move as international lawlessness.

Britain and France pleaded for peace. The British Prime Minister, Neville Chamberlain, desperate for peace at any price, asked Mussolini to persuade Hitler to stop aggression. The leaders of the four countries met at Munich, Germany, to confer on Hitler's demands. At this famous conference, the British and French appeased Hitler and gave in to his decision to occupy Czechoslovakia.

"This is the last territorial claim I have to make in Europe," Hitler told them, and they believed him. German tanks rumbled into Czechoslovakia without resistance.

FDR realized that this appeasement policy would only whet Hitler's appetite. He implored Chamberlain not to abandon Czechoslovakia and to maintain a strong stand. But he could only offer words of encouragement. Congress would not allow foreign alliances. After the Munich conference, the American people drew a breath of relief, wanting to believe Hitler's promises that the agreement meant permanent peace.

But in Britain one man assessed the situation more clearly. "We have sustained a total and unmitigated defeat," said Winston Churchill.

In FDR's message to Congress, January, 1939, he spoke somberly of the prospects for peace. "A war which threatened to envelop the world in flames has been averted; but it has become increasingly clear that world peace is not assured. . . . There comes a time in the affairs of men when they must prepare to defend, not their homes alone but the tenets of faith and humanity on which their churches, their governments and their very civilization are founded."

Before the snows of winter had melted, Hitler moved to take the rest of Czechoslovakia and turned his bullying threats toward Poland. Despite this overwhelming act of aggression and threat of war, great isolationist sentiment still remained. But FDR quietly and resolutely went about defending the country. He united the western hemisphere in a policy of mutual defense and provided financial aid to the beleaguered Chinese forces fighting against the Japanese on the China mainland.

In March, 1939, fascist forces struck again. Hitler had already seized all of Czechoslovakia. Japan invaded the Spratly Islands, thus threatening U.S. Philippine outposts. General Franco took Madrid in Spain. Mussolini seized Albania.

"Never in my life have I seen things moving in the world with more crosscurrents or with greater velocity." said Roosevelt. He wrote directly to the fascist dictators, sending them a list of thirty-one nations that he asked them not to attack. The Axis leaders ridiculed Roosevelt's naïve appeal for peace. In the United States, shortsighted isolationists gloated over this embarrassment to the President.

Once again Roosevelt tried to persuade Congress to repeal the Neutrality Act and tried to show clearly the dangers of war that advanced month by month. Isolationist leader Senator William E. Borah responded that he knew the future better than the President. "There's not going to be any war this year. All this hysteria is manufactured and artificial," he insisted.

Secretary Hull invited Senator Borah to the State Department to read cables pouring in from Europe predicting war. But Borah only replied, "I have sources of information in Europe that I regard as more reliable than those of the State Department."

Vice-President Garner confronted Roosevelt. "Well, Captain, we may as well face the fact. You haven't got the votes: and that's all there is to it." Smugly the isolationists assured themselves they had won another victory.

In August, 1939, another stunning blow fell upon the democracies. Gigantic Russia and powerful Germany signed a nonaggression pact not to wage war on each other. Germany was free now to pounce upon another victim, Poland, with the assurance that Russia would make no move to defend her neighbor.

The catastrophic news was announced at the White House at three o'clock in the morning. "Tony Biddle has just got through from Warsaw, Mr. President. Several German divisions are deep in Polish territory, and fighting is heavy." Anthony Drexel Biddle, the Ambassador to Poland, reported bombers

flying over Warsaw and then his line was discon-
nected.

"Well . . . it's come at last. God help us all," sighed
the President. He hung up his phone and summoned
his staff to the White House.

"We are ending our deathwatch over Europe,"
said Adolph Berle.

The next day came the swift tide of war. France
and England announced they would go to war if Hitler refused to withdraw his troops. On September 3,
1939, they honored their pledge to Poland.

"I have to tell you now that this country is at war
with Germany," the brokenhearted Prime Minister
Chamberlain told his stricken people. World War II
had begun.

Tanks and guns rumbled through Polish country-
side as Americans huddled around their radios to
hear the terrible news of the Nazi invasion.

Roosevelt talked to the anxious nation. "When
peace has been broken anywhere, the peace of all
countries everywhere is in danger," he warned. "This
nation will remain a neutral nation, but I cannot ask
that every American remain neutral."

Desperate appeals for aid poured in from the Allies, and everywhere across America people argued
and debated and fought over the possibility of entering the war. They agreed by now that America
must help the Allies, but they still could not agree to
war. Finally, over a month after the Nazi invasion,

after bitter controversy, Congress repealed the embargo on arms to permit Allied nations to purchase munitions for their defense. But this was strictly on a "cash and carry" basis; they had to pay in currency and transport the arms themselves, for American ships were still not permitted to take war materiel into battle zones.

After the *blitzkrieg* and division of the spoils of Poland by Germany on the west and Russia on the east, a tense period of quiet fell upon Europe. It was marred only by the invasion of tiny Finland by Russia; Finland put up a heroic battle but fell to the giant invader.

This was the winter of the "phony war," as the Americans thought. They were as overoptimistic as ever. They insisted that the Allies had called Hitler's bluff and that this foreign war would settle down to a long period of siege that they need not be dragged into.

An eerie silence fell over the White House. "Things here are amazingly quiet," wrote the President. In Europe one could see French and German trenches face to face, but not a gun was fired and no disturbance broke the stillness that winter.

Then in an April dawn, 1940, with a thunder of tanks and guns and bombs, Hitler struck again. German troops crossed the border of Denmark and emptied out of troopships along the coast of Norway.

Denmark fell in a few hours, Norway in a few weeks. At full speed the Germans turned and rolled over the Low Countries. Across the Dutch and Belgian frontiers swept dive bombers, infantry, and tanks.

Half a million Allied troops readied for battle behind Belgian lines. But superior German military might crushed the Allied armies and rolled into northern France.

Roosevelt, showing immense courage, serenity, and confidence to the shaken nation in this perilous moment of crisis, reacted calmly to this hurricane of events. He asked for almost a billion dollars of aid to the faltering Allies and fifty thousand planes a year to rush to the Allied defense. When Congress agreed, he asked for more.

Disaster after disaster befell the Allied armies as German military might pushed them back toward the English Channel. Retreating to Dunkirk, the battered British army was evacuated across the Channel. FDR somberly told the nation, "On this Sabbath evening, in our homes in the midst of our American families, let us calmly consider what we have done and what we must do." The nation must step up its defense, modernize its arms, enlarge its factories, he said. "Ours is a high duty, a noble task."

As France tottered on the brink of defeat, Italy joined in to divide the spoils by declaring war on France. On June 10 the President announced grimly,

"The hand that held the dagger has struck it into the back of its neighbor."

Frantic pleas for help from France were to no avail. In June, 1940, France fell. Only Britain in all of Western Europe was left to fight the Nazi hordes, and she herself could easily be flying the German swastika before the end of that tragic year.

The President did everything he could to help Britain short of actually declaring war. That summer as bombs rained down on England and waves of Nazi planes blackened the skies over the British Isles, FDR concluded agreements to provide Britain with U.S. destroyers in exchange for use of naval bases in the Caribbean and prepared to ask Congress for all-out partnership and lend-lease aid to Britain.

The American Army began to use stovepipes for practice cannons, cans as makeshift ammunition, and broomsticks as machine guns until more effective weapons could be produced. Congress passed the first compulsory peacetime draft in American history to raise an army of men to defend democracy.

Gradually, the country was being prepared for the inevitable conflict.

CHAPTER FOURTEEN

★ ★ ★ ★ ★ ★

AN UNPRECEDENTED THIRD TERM

Would he run again in 1940 or not? Everywhere, people asked the big question. Nobody knew the answer, not even the President himself. But all around the nation, people played the guessing game, assuming he himself had already made up his mind.

By 1940 the fieldstone library that housed the FDR papers at Hyde Park was completed, and his beautiful hilltop dream house was almost done. He planned on retiring there to write and put his papers in order. He was very tired.

He told Dan Tobin early in 1940, "I have to have a rest. I want to go home to Hyde Park. I want to take care of my trees. I have a big planting there, Dan. I want to make the farm pay. I want to finish my little house on the hill. I want to write history. No, I just can't do it, Dan."

It seemed very likely he would retire. In American history no other President had run for a third consecutive term, and Americans were not in favor of

such long power for one President. They were opposed not to this President himself but to the breaking of a solid American tradition. Yet Roosevelt had
never been more popular or his leadership more necessary, said the Democratic party. In this time of
crisis they appealed to him to run again.

Time and time again FDR told the party he had
no desire nor intention to run again. He repeated it
often enough for his own closest advisers, men like
Jim Farley, to believe him. During the winter of
1939, the time of the "phony war," when all seemed
calm in Europe, it was even more certain he would
retire.

Then came the deepening crisis, the German
"blitz" that spring of 1940, when all of Europe was
threatened and the foundations of democracy were
shaken. Now fear arose and with it the knowledge
that America must have a strong and courageous
hand on the government if it hoped to survive in the
critical times ahead.

At the Republican convention in June the collapse
of France dominated the news and the defense of the
United States became the primary issue. The Republicans picked out a bright new star as their candidate. Wendell L. Willkie was a big man with tousled
hair and a hearty laugh, who looked and talked like
an Indiana farm boy but was actually a top utilities
counsel. "A simple barefoot Wall Street lawyer,"

Harold Ickes called him, but he knew as did everyone else what a strong candidate Willkie was. He was not a reactionary, had supported many New Deal measures, and had accepted Roosevelt's internationalist foreign policy. Willkie was a perfect foil for FDR, eager for a tough fight and supremely confident that he would win the battle.

By July, when the Democratic convention convened in Chicago, the President had made up his mind, but few knew his decision. He had kept so silent on whether he would run again that newspapers drew caricatures of him as a sphinx. But as he watched the crisis in Asia and Europe darken that spring and summer, he knew he must run for the good of the nation. He insisted that the party clearly show their desire for him to be their leader. He wanted a clear mandate, a draft from the party, and he refused to take a leadership role at the convention.

It opened in Chicago in the heat of July, and the delegates were leaderless but imploring Roosevelt to run. Jim Farley wanted the nomination himself and set about securing votes. Cordell Hull and Garner had also voiced opposition to a third-term President and were rallying votes for themselves. The convention threatened to turn into chaos.

Finally, in the midst of the confusion of the second day, the permanent chairman, Senator Alben Barkley, delivered an important speech that Roosevelt had skillfully maneuvered, authorizing what Barkley said.

"The President has never had, and has not today, any desire or purpose to continue in the office of President, to be a candidate for that office, or to be nominated by the convention for that office. He wishes in all earnestness and sincerity to make it clear that all the delegates to this convention are free to vote for any candidate. That is the message I bear to you from the President of the United States."

There was a moment of uncertainty and silence.

Then everyone understood, and a tumultuous roar rocked the walls of the convention hall.

"WE WANT ROOSEVELT"
"WE WANT ROOSEVELT"
"EVERYBODY WANTS ROOSEVELT"

Impromptu parades formed, huge signs bobbed, and bands blared as the delegates shouted for their choice. The President's name was put up in nomination and the outcome was obvious. Roosevelt received 946 votes, Farley 72, and a few votes were scattered among the other nominees.

FDR had received his draft.

But the game was not completely won. He had decided that he would run only with a real, unquestioned New Deal Vice-Presidential candidate. He had chosen liberal New Dealer Henry Wallace and refused to consider any other selection. The Secretary of Agriculture was not a popular choice and tension mounted as the Vice-Presidential nominee was announced. The delegates were angered, feeling that Roosevelt was railroading in an unwanted candidate. In near mutiny, they hissed Wallace's name, but the President was adamant. No Wallace, no Roosevelt, he said firmly. In the end they voted for Wallace as Roosevelt wanted. Now the President could come before the delegates and accept the nomination.

"It is with a very full heart that I speak tonight. I must confess that I do so with mixed feelings—because I find myself, as almost everyone does sooner or later in his lifetime, in a conflict between deep personal desire for retirement on the one hand, and that quiet, invisible thing called 'conscience' on the other. . . . Today all private plans, all private lives, have been in a sense repealed by an overriding public danger. . . . Only the people themselves can draft a President. If such a draft should be made upon me, I say to you, in the utmost simplicity, I will, with God's help, continue to serve with the best of my ability and with the fullest of my strength."

The campaign of 1940 was a bitter battle for the Presidency. In his own inscrutable way, Roosevelt first insisted he would not campaign at all. "I shall not have the time nor the inclination to engage in purely political debate," he announced.

But Willkie attacked the New Deal tirelessly back and forth across the country in pounding speeches. Speaking day after day as he did, the Republican's voice grew husky, then hoarse, and finally became only a broken croak, but he continued to hammer away at Roosevelt.

First he called FDR an appeaser of the Fascists. When he saw the people would not respond to those charges, he changed his attack. Roosevelt was a warmonger. If Roosevelt were elected, we would be at war within six months, he cried, and this argument touched the critical nerve center of the people. They did not want war. Willkie had found the telling argument and he pounded away at Roosevelt, the dictator and warmonger, until the Democrats began nervously to beg Roosevelt to come out and fight.

Early in the campaign, defense problems were so demanding, FDR said, that he could not campaign at all. He spent his time inspecting shipyards and Army bases, where he had to pass through large cities and the masses could see and cheer their President. But Willkie's hoarse cries of warmonger grew more strident and even the mighty New York *Times* endorsed the Republican contender. FDR waited for the appropriate moment to wade in and slug it out in the campaign arena.

FDR always had a superb sense of political timing. He was a professional at the campaigning game and patiently bided his time until the precise moment when he could strike best. Finally, late in October, a few weeks before election day, when public opinion polls had begun to show Willkie cutting into the President's lead, he moved.

"I am an old campaigner and I love a good fight," he said with a broad grin.

He knew foreign policy was the key issue and here the people relied upon his experience over that of the unknown Willkie. To Willkie's cries of warmonger, FDR patiently replied, "I have said this before but I shall say it again and again and again: Your boys are not going to be sent into any foreign war."

The people listened and were convinced.

In the final results of the election, they supported Roosevelt and his foreign policy for a third term. Millions, more than had ever voted before, lined up at the polls and gave Roosevelt a decisive victory. He received more than twenty-seven million votes while his opponent received twenty-two million. In electoral votes he took 449 to Willkie's 82. At a moment of world crisis the people placed their trust in the strength Roosevelt had shown as America's leader.

While Americans were deciding who should be their leader, the *Luftwaffe*, the German air force, had not been idle. After the broken remains of the British army had been evacuated from Dunkirk to the British Isles, the *Luftwaffe* had begun its destruction of English cities. Day and night the English people suffered under the massive bombing. They were led by Winston Churchill, who said he had only blood, sweat, and tears to give, but also gave incredible courage to the besieged British people.

Americans read the terrible news of the air attacks on Britain and lost some of their neutrality. They still wanted to stay out of war, but now they openly prayed for the defeat of Germany and of its leader. In September, when Japan formed a partnership with Germany and Italy in a Tripartite Pact, Americans realized the pincer had formed on both sides of the United States. This would be a two-ocean war, and they agreed with Roosevelt that Britain must be kept going a little longer. Time was of the essence. We must do everything short of war to gain time for us to arm, Roosevelt said, and he proposed a two-ocean Navy, brought Republicans into his Cabinet to form a bipartisan group for war planning, and most important of all, created the lend-lease program to aid Britain.

Lend-lease committed America to pouring all available aid into Britain to help save her. The President asked Congress for power to spend seven billion dollars in lend-lease money to protect America. He proposed to lend goods rather than money.

Massive shipments of war supplies were sped across the Atlantic, but all too often they were torpedoed by waiting German U-boats and were sunk to the bottom of the ocean. The U.S. had to find a way to deal with the wolf packs of German submarines if lend-lease materials were to reach their goal. Roosevelt extended neutrality zones far out into the Atlantic, ordered locations of subs to be radioed to the waiting British navy, and by 1941, ordered convoys to be escorted to Iceland. America's Good Neighbor policy in Latin America was reinforced by new agreements for mutual hemispheric defense.

Then in June, 1941, Hitler's army struck again. Germany launched a massive surprise attack on its ally Russia, a thrust so powerful that fears were common that the Soviet Union would collapse within weeks. But the courageous Russian army refused to bend before the Nazi military machine, though German tanks rolled ever farther into the heartland of Russia toward Moscow. Roosevelt extended lend-lease to the Soviet Union to aid Russian resistance to the Nazi aggression.

Now it was more important than ever to patrol the seas. German U-boats struck again and again at merchant fleets. FDR ordered the Navy to fire on submarines on sight, and Congress voted to arm merchantmen and allow them to sail to belligerent ports. Naval war with Germany was now under way. Germany still had not declared war on the United States, and war did not come from the European continent first. The Pacific Ocean, rather than the Atlantic, would be the scene of the attack that propelled the United States into world war.

Throughout the past decade the Japanese on their

march of conquest through Asia had seized every opportunity for aggression. They believed American concern with European affairs would prevent the President from dealing with Asian conquest. By summer of 1939 Japan had forced the United States to announce that it would cut off by January, 1940, critical shipments of oil, scrap iron, and raw materials vital to their war machine.

The hope was that this action would deter Japan from further conquest, since the United States supplied the Japanese with over half the supplies needed to wage war. FDR's advisers cautioned against a complete embargo on war materials in order to avoid a showdown. But when the United States finally denied Japan tin, rubber, scrap iron, and steel, war with Japan came ever closer.

The Japanese government said they wanted to negotiate over this embargo and sent Prince Konoye to discuss concessions with FDR.

Tension mounted steadily. Japanese warlords had announced intentions of moving in on the Philippines, Malaya, and Indonesia. They had already built airfields in Indochina, and by summer had seized helpless French Indochina. FDR knew he must move with determination to show Japan that America would not tolerate such aggression.

He received the Philippine armed forces into the U.S. Army. He appointed General Douglas MacArthur to the command of the Far East. He froze Japanese financial assets in the United States and cut off all supplies of rubber, scrap iron, and fuel oil. It was this embargo that brought the two countries to the point of war in the minds of the Japanese generals who needed these vital raw materials.

Now time was critical. Both governments believed war was only a matter of time. Japan wanted time to consolidate her military might. The United States wanted time to fortify the Philippines and strengthen the Navy. General Tojo, Japan's war minister, felt confident Japan would win over America. He presented a final ultimatum: Japan would occupy no more Asian territory if the United States would stop arming the Philippines, cut off aid to China, and unfreeze Japanese assets in the U.S. Of course, he knew his demands were impossible and that the United States could not agree. In secret he planned a full-scale sneak attack.

On November 26, 1941, an enormous Japanese striking force of carriers, airplanes, battleships, heavy cruisers, and destroyers headed out to sea from its secret rendezvous in the Kurile Islands. As they headed south, war was imminent.

But no word of the tremendous convoy leaked out. Ships and troop-carrying transports had been spotted steaming south through the China Sea, and warning messages sped across the Pacific. They alerted the government of the possibility of an attack in the Philippines, Thailand, or the Malay Peninsula. But the true target of the Japanese navy was elsewhere.

Nobody in Washington really believed that Japan, no matter how belligerent, would be so foolhardy as to attack American territory directly and incite the country into full-scale war. As top military brass wondered what Japan was planning, General Tojo ordered the sneak attack that he hoped would destroy the entire Pacific fleet, even before war was officially declared between the two countries.

On the morning of December 7 Americans slept as a morning mist covered the naval base at Pearl Harbor, Hawaii. Calm and serene, all the important ships of the Pacific fleet lay at anchor, side by side, sitting ducks for an attack. At 7:55 A.M. the first wave of Japanese airplanes dropped bombs upon the fleet and rained aerial torpedoes on waiting targets. A second wave followed an hour later.

Three minutes after the first raid the tragic message speeded across the ocean.

AIR RAID, PEARL HARBOR—THIS IS NO DRILL

This was the "day that shall live in infamy" said President Roosevelt. Almost twenty-five hundred American sailors, soldiers, marines, and civilians lost their lives, and over a thousand more were wounded. One hundred and forty-nine American planes were lost on the ground or water. The battleships *Arizona* and *Oklahoma* capsized, and other battleships were destroyed or badly damaged.

Simultaneously, on airfields near Manila, most of the B-17 planes stationed there were destroyed; Japan landed troops on the Malay Peninsula, and Guam was bombed.

The sneak attack was far more successful than Japan realized. The United States was rendered paralyzed and almost helpless in the Pacific and experienced the most formidable defeat in its history. But the incredible news of disaster that day angered and unified the American people. Finally they were solidly behind their President, who had warned so long and so earnestly that the country must be prepared for global conflict.

Congress declared war against Japan on December 8. Germany and Italy declared war on the United States three days later.

As America went to war, the President said grimly, "Never before has there been a greater challenge to life, liberty, and civilization."

CHAPTER FIFTEEN

★ ★ ★ ★ ★ ★

THE COURAGEOUS WARRIOR

"Hostilities exist," said the President. "We are in it."

The first months of war were the darkest America had ever faced. In 1942, during the winter and spring after Pearl Harbor, the United States suffered one humiliating defeat after another. With one mighty blow Japan had annihilated much of the Pacific fleet, but fortunately Japan did not realize how defenseless the United States was.

After Pearl Harbor there was little sea, air, or land power available to stop the Japanese advance. Guam fell, then Wake Island, and next Hong Kong. Singapore in Malaya surrendered in February, the East Indies in March, and Burma in April. In the Philippine Islands, exhausted American and Philippine troops under the leadership of General Douglas MacArthur put up a gallant fight for survival but were pushed to a last-ditch stand on Bataan. On that remote peninsula many brave Americans gave their lives for their country. The last American flag still flying in the Far East was finally surrendered on the island of Corregidor in Manila Bay, after a prolonged and heroic defense. Retreat, disaster, and retreat were the news from the Pacific. Only Australia and India were left as bulwarks against the domination of all of the Far East by Japan.

These were days of supreme emergency, and the President showed the courage, confidence, and tireless energy that would serve as a model to all the nation in the grim days of war. It was his role to lead once again, as he had in the darkest hours of 1933. This time the survival of the nation was at stake.

The President marshaled every resource to fight the war. His political life had been a training ground for this moment. "Dr. Win-the-War" had replaced "Dr. New Deal," he said, and he threw all the nation's energy into the battle.

His job was to turn the United States into a machine for waging total war, and this he did. He had already established war production plans with the lend-lease program before Pearl Harbor. He knew that soon the industrial might of the nation would be churning out materials necessary for the war.

Planning boards for defense, production, and price and supply controls were created. He tackled the enormous task of setting up networks of agencies and finding good men to run them. Tirelessly and cheerfully he mediated between many conflicting points of view to avoid stalemates and bickering in Washington. There were lags and shortcomings and confusion. But the job got done.

Soon the defense industry gathered momentum, and airplanes, ships, guns, uniforms, and tanks began to pour out of defense plants that were running night and day. The War Production Board accelerated production, and once the defense industry was organized, it produced war materials in quantities the enemy could not hope to equal.

FDR created the War Manpower Commission to organize the labor force efficiently, and women began to work in defense jobs as their husbands and sons went off to war. Salaries went up, and the dangers of inflation became serious. Boards had to be set up to regulate wages and prices. As shortages began to develop, FDR ordered rationing on such items as tires, sugar, gas, coffee, meat, canned foods, butter, and shoes.

In order to catch up with German scientific achievements, the President had already created a scientific committee to do research for the government. Now this Office of Scientific Research and Development brought together scientific talent to help win the war.

Roosevelt had shown great foresight and vision in encouraging scientific experiment. Enrico Fermi, the physicist, and Albert Einstein, the mathematician, had sent word to him that German scientists had successfully achieved atomic fission in uranium. Nazi scientists seemed on their way to producing the first atomic bomb. Roosevelt immediately realized the vast implications of these experiments in nuclear fission. He set a group of scientists to the task of catching up with the Germans. Within months the Manhattan Project was born, and the government secretly poured two billion dollars into this project on the gamble to produce an atomic bomb. In 1942 the first controlled chain reaction occurred in an atomic pile at the University of Chicago.

So the nation girded its resources of men, material, and spirit to win the war. By the end of the fighting, war production was so efficient that the output of the defense industry was double that of all the Axis powers combined.

It had always been Roosevelt's deepest hope that his contribution to history would be to help achieve a lasting peace throughout the world. He had watched Wilson's failure with the League of Nations after the first war and he was determined to avoid those mistakes. In his message to Congress in 1941 he was already working out ideas for a better world where the "four freedoms" should be guaranteed to all. The freedoms he spoke of were Freedom of Religion, Freedom of Speech, Freedom from Want, and Freedom from Fear.

Early in 1942 FDR and Churchill met in Newfoundland. This was the famous Atlantic Charter conference where they talked over their ideas on postwar reconstruction and devised a fair system for peace settlements. The Atlantic Charter shows clearly the hopes of both leaders for a better world based on freedom, respect for peoples, and security among nations.

The two world leaders of democracy met many times during the war. During those conferences they developed a confidence, mutual trust, and friendship rare among modern leaders. Their relationship grew in depth and strength, and because of this, diplomatic relations between the two major Allied powers were close and cordial.

At the outset of war FDR's military advisers, the Joint Chiefs of Staff, had decided that Germany rather than Japan must be the first target to defeat. This decision was prompted by the fact that Germany had a superior military force, bigger war production, and German scientists were deeply involved in inventing powerful secret weapons capable of immense destruction. So the President ordered an all-out German offensive as soon as possible. In the meantime, he decreed that aid to the Allies, Great Britain and Russia, must be increased as rapidly as possible until America's armies could be built up.

The greatest obstacle to shipping supplies to the Allies were the wolf packs of German submarines lurking in Atlantic waters to prey upon passing convoys. Time after time freighters and tankers were destroyed by U-boats even along America's Atlantic coastline. German U-boat captains became so bold that they began to torpedo vessels only thirty miles out from New York Harbor, and Americans could see the telltale smoke of burning oil tankers from the mainland.

Under FDR's pushing, America worked hard to build its own fleet. "Sixty vessels in sixty days" became the production slogan. With massive effort, sixty-seven ships were actually produced in one sixty-day period. A convoy system was soon worked out for the production of ships, but throughout the bleak year of 1942 marauding German subs stalked their victims almost without interference.

During the first summer of war in 1942 events were heartbreaking. The first German front shifted to North Africa, where the German Afrika Korps, a bold and capable striking force, had stopped the British army in Libya. FDR and Churchill met in Washington in June to set a date for a Second Front invasion. Stalin demanded immediate action. He wanted an invasion on a Second Front in Europe, for his nation was bearing the brunt of German armies on the Eastern Front. FDR agreed with Stalin on a cross-channel invasion into France, but he knew it could not be undertaken until men and materials were ready. Churchill pushed for a North African campaign first, and that June he and FDR planned the invasion of North Africa as a first step to help their desperate Russian ally.

Meanwhile, on the Japanese front in 1942, before America could take the offensive, the war situation looked bleak. The Japanese controlled all of East Asia and looked hungrily toward Australia and India. Never before in history had there been so quick a series of conquests, and if Japan continued her successful warfare and took India, she might actually unite in the Middle East with her other partners in the Axis.

In May, 1942, the Battle of the Coral Sea was fought off the northern coast of Australia. This was the first encounter in naval warfare history to be fought exclusively with planes operating from aircraft carriers. Here after a vicious air battle the Japanese forces were stopped for the first time. The Americans had thwarted Japan's plans to seize Australia.

Japan then turned toward Midway Island, Hawaii's strategic western outpost vital to Japanese plans to capture Pearl Harbor. The enemy did not know that before the Battle of Midway, American intelligence had cracked the secret Japanese code and could intercept and translate messages. U.S. naval strategy for the Battle of Midway was planned accordingly, catching the Japanese flat-footed. American forces gained one of the decisive victories of the

Pacific War. Danger of invasion of Hawaii and the Pacific coast by Japan was averted. The United States achieved containment in the Pacific, and now could carry on defensive action until troops and war materials were gathered for an offensive war.

In January, 1943, Roosevelt and Churchill met again, this time at Casablanca. They discussed the strategy of the invasion of Sicily and settled on a formula for the unconditional surrender of Axis powers. By unconditional surrender they meant the defeat of fascist powers intent on conquest and subjugation of other people. But FDR and Churchill insisted that unconditional surrender should not require the destruction of the population of Germany, Italy, and Japan.

Though the British and American leaders had developed a trusting partnership, they had failed to find a common meeting ground with the Soviet leader, Joseph Stalin, who remained distrustful of their every move and refused to attend their conferences. FDR had poured lend-lease aid into the Eastern Front and had pushed the North African campaign as quickly as possible to show his faith, but Stalin remained antagonistic and insisted that Russia still bore the brunt of the war effort against Germany. FDR and Churchill discussed ways to win the suspicious Soviet leader's confidence. It was easier to agree on war strategy than on political considerations among the Big Three, they realized, but they knew that lasting peace had to be built on more than military victories.

In early 1943 the Allied troops in North Africa began to push the Germans out. The Afrika Korps, led by brilliant German General Erwin Rommel, had fought the British army to a standstill in Libya in 1942 and had crushed them at El Alamein. But now as a stepping-stone for an invasion of southern Europe, Allied forces invaded Morocco and Algeria. They continued to Tunisia where hard-fought battles brought defeat to the Germans. By May, 1943, all the Axis forces in Africa were beaten. Now invasion of Italy, the "soft underbelly of Europe," was ensured.

Meanwhile, in the Pacific the American forces were beginning to achieve victory. They had taken the offensive late in 1942. The first big target was Guadalcanal in the Solomon Islands, where the Japanese were building an air base to attack Australia. The fighting on Guadalcanal was long, bloody, and costly. Heroic American troops fought in malarial jungles and swamps in bitter combat. It took six long months of desperate fighting and heavy losses of men to take the vital island. But with its victory in early 1943, the United States came closer to winning the Pacific War.

The summer of 1943 marked a turning point of the war in Europe and the Pacific. The successful invasion of Sicily was a rehearsal for the later massive invasion of Normandy. Next Allied troops invaded

the Italian mainland. A prolonged campaign was
waged by the Germans, but in fierce combat American soldiers slowly pushed the Nazis northward.

Throughout the entire war the United States
wrestled with the problem of submarines, but gradually huge convoys were assembled, and they were
protected by anti-submarine vessels, air patrols, new
radar devices, and escort carriers. By September,
1943, the Allies had German submarines under better
control, and they were shipping men and supplies
across the Atlantic with less interference.

Late in 1943 FDR and Churchill were able to persuade Stalin to meet with them to discuss war and
peace. They hoped to promote goodwill and cement
a firmer relationship with Stalin. The meeting of the
Big Three was held in Teheran, Iran, chosen for its
convenience to the Russian leader. Stalin had not set
foot outside of Russia for thirty years, and some believed he had never flown in an airplane. No President of the United States had ever traveled so far for
a conference, but the courageous warrior, crippled
and overworked, nevertheless was willing to hurdle
any obstacle and endure any hardship if only he
could promote his long-range objective of winning a
lasting peace.

The meeting at Teheran was the friendliest of any
meetings with the difficult Russian leader. "We are
going to get along fine with him and the Russian

people—very well indeed," the optimistic American President said.

The Big Three discussed ways of keeping Germany from becoming too powerful after the war and fixed a date for the invasion of France. The atmosphere seemed to be one of mutual trust and cordiality, and neither FDR nor Churchill doubted Russia's good faith.

Later on, they would find their trust had been misplaced. Just a few weeks after the pleasant talks, the American Ambassador in Moscow wired, "The Russian Bear is demanding much and yet biting the hands that are feeding it."

CHAPTER SIXTEEN

★★★★★★

THE FINAL CAMPAIGN

The invasion of Normandy was set for June, 1944, the greatest amphibious assault ever attempted. A force of almost three million men had gathered in southern England to await the D-day signal. "This mighty host," said their commander, General Dwight D. Eisenhower, "was as tense as a . . . great human spring, coiled for the moment when its energy should be released."

The Battle of Normandy lasted for six grim weeks. Hitler's defenses were massive, but by the end of the engagement, German generals were ready to negotiate for a separate peace. Hitler, however, was determined never to surrender, and so the war continued.

Slowly the Allied armies advanced through France. Paris was liberated in August, and the Allies stood poised to invade Germany. Hitler had lost almost half a million men but would not surrender.

In the Pacific campaign, American troops invaded

Japanese-held territories, island by island, and the names of these tiny outposts still remain as memorials to valiant Americans fighting and dying for their country. Bougainville, Tarawa, Kiska, Attu, Truk, and Saipan were taken one by one.

Politics did not stop in 1944 even though the war continued. It was the year for another Presidential election.

In the House the Republicans had increased their strength in the off-year election in 1942. Now in 1944 they had high hopes of beating Roosevelt at last. They picked as his opponent Thomas E. Dewey, governor of New York, the office FDR once held. A dynamic and personable man, Dewey adopted an internationalist foreign policy and accepted the most important New Deal reforms. Republicans thought that if anyone could oust the Democrats, Dewey could.

A fourth-term nomination for the Presidency was Roosevelt's if he wanted it, since he had already broken the precedent. But FDR was a weary man. The strain of being a wartime President had taken its toll on him.

He said, "All that is within me cries out to go back to my home on the Hudson River," but he agreed to run if asked. He could not turn his back on the responsibilities of seeing the war through and helping construct a lasting peace for the world.

The Democrats chose him, of course, with the

slogan that "we cannot change horses in the middle of the stream." To placate the party, FDR had to sacrifice Henry Wallace as his running mate and accept the party's choice of Harry S. Truman.

At first the campaign seemed dull, for FDR refused to enter into the fray, even though the energetic Dewey waged a vigorous battle. Over and over Dewey accused those "tired and quarrelsome old men" of the Democratic party of incompetence and inefficiency. It was time for a change, he cried.

Looking old and wan, and losing weight now, FDR was obviously fatigued from his years of overwork. Talk persisted about his poor health, especially when he limited his campaigning to inspection trips. The Republicans grew bolder in their speeches. In one speech they taunted Roosevelt about his beloved pet dog, Fala. They accused him of sending a destroyer all the way to the Aleutian Islands at taxpayer's expense just to pick up the little dog.

At this charge the President's temper was aroused.

"I am accustomed to hearing malicious falsehoods about myself—such as that old worm-eaten chestnut that I have represented myself as indispensable. But I think I have a right to resent, to object to libelous statements about my dog," he said. He counterattacked with relish, as if happy to be back in battle at last. The people seemed glad to have him in old form and began to laugh at Dewey.

But talk of Roosevelt's declining health continued,

and polls began to show Republicans closing the gap. FDR realized he must exert his old charm and physical strength by campaigning during the few weeks before election day. He proved his stamina just before election when he spent a day riding around in an open car in a heavy rainstorm. At the end of the day the President was drenched and exhausted, and his aides all worried over him. But he had proved his point to the nation.

The people needed his guidance and voted for him once again. They gave him a three-and-a-half-million-vote majority over Dewey. The electoral vote was 432 to 99. Franklin Delano Roosevelt was asked to continue to hold the reins of world leadership for a fourth term.

Roosevelt's fourth inaugural address was given at the White House, rather than the Capitol, to save his time and strength. He spoke for only a few minutes, but he addressed himself to his main area of concern, an international peace. "In the days and years that are to come," he said, "we shall work for a just and honorable peace, a durable peace, as today we work and fight for total victory in war."

He had always insisted that the paramount hope for a lasting peace must be through a powerful international organization. For many years he had dreamed of a new League of Nations, a "united nations." Early in the war he had set his Secretary of State, Cordell Hull, to the task of promoting a bipartisan foreign policy aimed at the eventual adoption of a world government.

The moment of its creation was coming closer. At Dumbarton Oaks in Washington in 1944 the general outline for such an organization had been planned. This significant conference produced the foundation of the United Nations.

The Big Three had not settled on all the details of the proposed United Nations, but they agreed that in time all nations should belong and that responsibility for safeguarding the peace should rest with the "four policemen"—the four wartime Allies, the United States, Great Britain, Russia, and China.

In February, 1945, shortly after FDR began his fourth term, the Big Three met again, this time at the Crimean resort of Yalta on the Black Sea. At Yalta, Churchill, Roosevelt, and Stalin decided several vital issues. Some of these decisions brought more criticism and dispute than any others of the war.

They discussed solutions to the problems of setting up the United Nations, talked over the sensitive question of how to set up peacetime governments for Poland and other liberated European countries, agreed to the partition of Germany, and debated possible Russian participation in the Far Eastern war.

FDR felt that continued cooperation among the major powers was of vital importance. For this reason he was willing to make certain concessions to Joseph Stalin. He agreed to a free election in Poland and to the establishment of interim governments in the other liberated countries to be followed by free elections. Unfortunately, this concession led to the establishment of communist satellite governments in those nations after the war.

The President's military advisers had insisted it was imperative that Russia enter the war against Japan for it was likely to drag on for a long time. Roosevelt, therefore, unnecessarily gave to the Soviet Union a great foothold in the Far East in exchange for her participation in the Japanese war. Germany was divided into four occupation zones, and the fate of Berlin was settled.

The Yalta Conference seemed to mark a new era of understanding and international peace. However, Roosevelt had prematurely placed his trust in the sincerity of the Soviet government without insisting on clearly defined terms. Perhaps it is fortunate that he did not live to witness the ultimate climate of Cold War that followed Yalta.

By mid-March, 1945, Churchill wrote unhappily to the American President of the "great failure and utter breakdown of what was settled at Yalta." It seemed that peace would not truly be secured.

But the President remained optimistic. "I came from the Crimea Conference with the firm belief that we have made a good start on the road to world peace," he said before Congress.

In military terms, victory seemed imminent. After a bitter winter of battle, Russia on the Eastern Front marched westward toward Berlin, while the Western powers moved steadily through Germany toward the capital. German cities shook under constant bombardment, and the Nazi tide slowly receded.

In the Pacific, the Japanese stronghold of Iwo Jima was captured in March, 1945, after vicious fighting. On Easter Sunday, 1945, amphibious forces landed on Okinawa to begin a three-month battle for the indispensable base. Slowly, with amphibious landings and air and sea assaults on these islands, America came closer to defeating Japan.

In March, the President made his last appearance before Congress. His hair had grown white and lines now etched his thinning face. During the winter he had suffered through a severe cold and for the first time had not bounced back with his usual vitality. He was tired and had hollows in his pale cheeks. His clothes hung loosely and at times his alert blue eyes seemed a bit clouded over.

He had seemed somewhat rested, though, after the cruise home from Yalta. Frances Perkins saw him and had written: "That Roosevelt man is a wonder. He gets tired, but just give him a little rest and a sea voyage and he comes right up again."

On March 29 he left Washington for a month's vacation at his beloved Warm Springs, which he had visited rarely during the war years. He desperately needed this time of relaxing in the sun and swimming in the warm waters of the pool. He mulled over plans and preparations for the realization of his greatest dream, the official creation of the United Nations, which would take place at San Francisco in a few weeks. He was to deliver the opening address and brought a draft of the speech with him to Warm Springs.

It was a warm and sunny Georgia afternoon on April 12. At his cottage the President was sitting in front of the fireplace, his cape draped about him, as an artist worked on his portrait. As he sat, he looked over the United Nations' speech he was preparing.

"The only limit to our realization of tomorrow will be our doubts of today," he had written. "Let us move forward with strong and active faith."

Suddenly, he stopped reading. He pressed his hand to his temple and rubbed for a moment at his neck. Then he said, "I have a terrific headache."

Those in the room looked up and rushed to him as he slumped over, unconscious. They called for doctors, who tried to revive the President. But their efforts were to no avail. Roosevelt had suffered a massive cerebral hemorrhage and never regained consciousness. Four hours after the attack he was dead.

Eleanor was called to Warm Springs. She sent the news to her children. "Darlings: Pa slept away this afternoon. He did his job to the end as he would want you to do. Bless you. All our love, Mother."

A stunned and mourning nation wept for its lost leader as the funeral train brought the President back to Washington. In the East Room of the White House the family gathered for a simple service. Then the President's coffin was carried slowly by train along the oft-taken route out of the capital city, through New York City, and then along the banks of the Hudson River to Hyde Park.

Franklin Delano Roosevelt was returning home for the last time to lay at rest among the shade trees, green lawns, and tranquil fields of the estate he loved so well. The aristocrat from the Hudson was home at last. And the small and the poor and the weak cried along with the great for the friend they had lost.

EPILOGUE

Death snatched away from Franklin Delano Roosevelt the chance to see the fulfillment of much of his work. He did not live to see peace come to Europe and Asia, nor the birth of the United Nations, nor the dawn of the nuclear age. All these events, which Roosevelt had worked so hard to achieve, occurred within a few months after he died.

Through the month of April, 1945, the Allied armies swept eastward over Germany, and victory seemed assured. On April 29 Hitler committed suicide in Berlin. On May 2 Berlin capitulated to the Russians while the remaining German troops in Italy and Austria gave in to American forces. On May 7 Hitler's successor, Admiral Doenitz, surrendered unconditionally to General Eisenhower, and the next day, May 8, was officially declared V–E Day. Victory in Europe was complete.

A month later, and two months after FDR's death, another of his hopes came to reality when representatives of fifty nations met in San Francisco to discuss an international organization to preserve world peace. On June 26, 1945, the fifty countries signed the United Nations Charter, which sought to "maintain international peace and security . . . to develop friendly relations among nations based on respect for the principle of equal rights and self-determination of peoples . . . to achieve international cooperation in solving international problems of an economic, social, cultural, or humanitarian character. . . ."

In July another Big Three conference was held, this time at Potsdam, Germany, where President Truman took the place so often held by FDR to discuss matters with Churchill and Stalin. This final war conference established terms of peace in Europe. And on July 26 the United States, Great Britain, and China signed the Potsdam Declaration calling for the surrender of Japan and setting the terms for peace in Asia.

The next day Japan broadcast her refusal of the Potsdam Declaration. She would not surrender.

Truman and Churchill had decided at Potsdam to use the atomic bomb if necessary for Japan's surrender, rather than prolong the war. On August 6 the first nuclear device was dropped on Hiroshima. Three days later a larger bomb was dropped on Nagasaki. The destruction in both cities was catastrophic, and the world stood horror-struck at the power that had been unleashed. The nuclear age had dawned.

Almost immediately, Japan agreed to most of the Potsdam Declaration for surrender, and the terms were worked out by August 17. September 2 was declared V–J Day. World War II was at an end.

The principles that Roosevelt had fought for in the thirties and early forties were continued in the post-war years by Democrats and Republicans alike struggling to regain prosperity at home and maintain peace and equilibrium abroad. In the years that followed, Eleanor Roosevelt became an international ambassador for humanitarian causes, carrying on the work that her husband, the thirty-second President of the United States, had fought for so long and so well.

Franklin D. Roosevelt had led the United States through two of the greatest crises of the twentieth century, the Great Depression and World War II. The aristocrat from the banks of the Hudson had become the man of the people, providing food and shelter for the destitute, jobs for the unemployed, and hope for the little man. Although crippled, he had become a man of strength and courage, carrying the nation through its fiercest war to a position of world leadership. And so his place in history is secure.

★★★★★★

CHRONOLOGY

1882   Franklin Delano Roosevelt born, Hyde Park, New York, January 30.

1896   Enters Groton School. Gives first political speech with debate team.

1898   Battles scarlet fever. Acquires *New Moon*.

1899   Theodore Roosevelt, his uncle, becomes governor of New York. Franklin joins Missionary Society.

1900   Enters Harvard College. James Roosevelt dies, December 8.

1901   Franklin travels in Europe with his mother. Theodore Roosevelt becomes President after William McKinley is assassinated.

1904   Appointed editor in chief of Harvard *Crimson*. Courts Eleanor. Graduates from Harvard. Enters Columbia University Law School.

1905   Marries Eleanor, March 17. Travel in Europe.

1906   Anna Eleanor Roosevelt born, May 3.

1907   Passes New York State bar examination. Joins law firm of Carter, Ledyard, and Milburn. James born, December 23.

1909   Franklin Delano, Jr., born March 18, died November.

1910   Elected state senator from Dutchess County. Moves to Albany. Fight with Tammany Hall. Elliott Roosevelt born, September 23.

1912   Re-elected state senator. Appointed Assistant Secretary of the Navy.

1914   Franklin Delano, Jr., born August 17.

1916   John Aspinwall born, March 13.

1917   President Wilson gives war message to Congress, April 20.

1919   Theodore Roosevelt dies, January 6. Franklin travels to Europe.

1920   Becomes Vice-Presidential nominee to run with James Cox at Democratic convention in San Francisco. Resigns from Navy to campaign.

1921   Appointed vice-president of Fidelity and Deposit Company of Maryland. Struck by poliomyelitis in August.

1924   Enters law partnership with Basil O'Connor. Becomes Alfred Smith's Presidential campaign manager.

1927   Enters Warm Springs, Georgia, resort for mineral-water treatments.

1928 Elected governor of New York.

1929 Stock market crashes, October.

1930 Re-elected governor of New York.

1932 Elected President of the United States.

1933 First Hundred Days: enacts New Deal philosophy in programs such as the Civilian Conservation Corps, Federal Emergency Relief Act, National Industrial Recovery Act, Agriculture Adjustment Act, Tennessee Valley Authority, and others.

1935 Enacts Social Security Act. Neutrality Act enacted. Italy invades Ethiopia.

1936 Re-elected President of the United States.

1937 Neutrality Act renewed. Quarantine Speech, October.

1938 Germany begins conquest of Europe.

1940 Re-elected for third term. National emergency recognized because of Axis aggression.

1941 Russia attacked by Germany. Pearl Harbor attacked, December 7. Congress declares war on Japan, December 8. Germany and Italy declare war on United States, December 11.

1942 Creates many war-time offices and commissions to speed the war effort, such as War Manpower Commission, Office of Price Stabilization, Office of Scientific Research and Development, and others. Manhattan Project succeeds—first controlled chain reaction at the University of Chicago. Battle of the Coral

Sea. Meets with Churchill in Washington in June.

1943   Meets with Churchill in Casablanca, in January. Meets with Churchill and Stalin in Teheran, Iran, in November.

1944   Battle of Normandy. Roosevelt re-elected for fourth term.

1945   Meets with Churchill and Stalin in Yalta, Crimea, in February, to plan the final defeat of Germany, and the establishment of the United Nations. Franklin Delano Roosevelt dies, April 12.

FOR FURTHER READING

Asbell, Bernard. *When F.D.R. Died*. New York: Holt, Rinehart and Winston, 1961.

Burns, James MacGregor. *Roosevelt: The Lion and the Fox*. New York: Harcourt, Brace & World, 1956.

Churchill, Allen. *The Roosevelts: American Aristocrats*. New York: Harper, 1965.

Douglas, Helen Gahagan. *The Eleanor Roosevelt We Remember*. New York: Hill & Wang, 1963.

Farley, James A. *Behind the Ballots*. New York: Harcourt, Brace & World, 1938.

Fenichell, Stephen S. *The United Nations Design For Peace*. New York: Holt, Rinehart and Winston, 1960.

Flynn, Edward J. *You're the Boss*. New York: Viking Press, 1947.

Freidel, Frank. *Franklin D. Roosevelt*. Boston: Little, Brown, 1952, 1954, 1956, 3 vols.

Gould, Jean. *A Good Fight—The Story of F.D.R.'s Conquest of Polio*. New York: Dodd, Mead, 1960.

Gunther, John. *Roosevelt in Retrospect: A Profile In History*. New York: Harper, 1950.

Hoover, Herbert. *The Memoirs of Herbert Hoover*. Vol. III, *The Great Depression, 1929-1941*. New York: Macmillan, 1952.

Ickes, Harold L. *The Secret Diary of Harold L. Ickes*. New York: Simon and Schuster, 1953-54, 3 vols.

Leuchtenberg, William E. *Franklin D. Roosevelt and the New Deal, 1932-1940*. New York: Harper, 1963.

Lindley, Ernest K. *Franklin D. Roosevelt, A Career in Progressive Democracy*. Indianapolis: Bobbs-Merrill, 1931.

MacLeish, Archibald. *The Eleanor Roosevelt Story*. Boston: Houghton Mifflin, 1965.

Moley, Raymond. *The First New Deal*. New York: Harcourt, Brace & World, 1966.

Perkins, Dexter. *The New Age of Franklin D. Roosevelt*. Chicago: The University of Chicago Press, 1957.

Perkins, Frances. *The Roosevelt I Knew*. New York: Viking Press, 1946.

Rauch, Basil, editor. *Franklin D. Roosevelt: Selected Speeches, Messages, Press Conferences, and Letters*. New York: Holt, Rinehart and Winston, 1957.

Richberg, Donald R. *My Hero*. New York: G. P. Putnam's Sons, 1954.

Rollins, Alfred B., Jr. *Roosevelt and Howe*. New York: Alfred A. Knopf, 1962.

Roosevelt, Eleanor. *This I Remember*. New York: Harper, 1949.

————. *This Is My Story*. New York: Harper, 1937.

Roosevelt, Elliott, editor. *FDR: His Personal Letters*. New York: Duell, Sloan and Pearce, 1950, 3 vols.

Roosevelt, James, and Shalett, Sidney. *Affectionately, F.D.R.: A Son's Story of a Lonely Man*. New York: Harcourt, Brace & World, 1959.

Roosevelt, Sara Delano. *My Boy Franklin*. New York: Ray Long and Richard R. Smith, 1933.

Rosenman, Samuel I. *Working with Roosevelt*. New York: Harper, 1952.

Schlesinger, Arthur M., Jr. *The Age of Roosevelt*. Boston: Houghton Mifflin, 1957, 1959, 1960, 3 vols.

Sherwood, Robert E. *Roosevelt and Hopkins*. New York: Harper, 1948.

Tugwell, Rexford G. *The Democratic Roosevelt*. Garden City, N.Y.: Doubleday, 1957.

Tully, Grace. *FDR: My Boss*. New York: Charles Scribner's Sons, 1949.

INDEX